Kost
National Poet of Hellas

Twelve Narratives of the Gypsy

Translation copyright © Manolis Aligizakis 2024
Published in 2024 by:
Libros Libertad Publishing Ltd
2244 154A Street, Surrey B.C. V4A 5S9

All rights reserved.
No part of this book may be reproduced
in any form without the written permission
of the publisher, with the exception of brief
passages in reviews.
Any request for photocopying or other
reproduction of any part of this book
should be directed in writing to the publisher
or to ACCESS:
The Canadian Copyright Licensing Agency,
One Yonge Street, Suite 800, Toronto, Ontario, Canada,
M5E 1E5.

ISBN: 9798325078002

Printed and bound with KDP

Kostis Palamas
National Poet of Hellas

Twelve Narratives
of the Gypsy

Translated by Manolis Aligizakis
Introduced by Georgia Kritikos

Libros Libertad

FOREWORD

The most prominent modern Hellene poet between the 1870ies and to the middle of the twentieth century Kostis Palamas, stands unchallenged in the Hellenic pantheon of Modern Poets; his long career spanned several decades and culminated in his being named the National Poet of Hellas. His contribution to Modern Hellenic poetry, inspired by both the Neo-Hellene poetic tradition and contemporary European trends, was immense and his work varied widely in form and mood as well as in subject matter, which ranged from everyday life events to esoteric views of the Hellenic psyche, to historical events, and to international issues and trends.

Kostis Palamas wrote a wide variety of poems, long and short, rhyming and free versed poems but his most serious works were two epic-lyric collections, *The King's Flute* and *Twelve Narratives of the Gypsy*, works which are read and studied even today, as they still provide insights into today's events and conditions in Hellas. As a leading proponent of the Greek literary renewal envisioned by the so-called generation of 1880, Palamas, fully aware of his leading role, undertook, in addition to renewing the interpretation of the Hellenic literary tradition, the renewal of the literary horizon, which presupposed the emergence of new poets. He embraced newcomers such as John Papadiamantopoulos, Nikos Kampas, and George Drossinis, promoting their work through positive reviews, and as a result became the living consciousness of a whole new generation of poets. Drossinis' verses are characterized by lively use of rhythm and rhyme. Elements of European Romanticism still remain despite many other departures from the poetics of the old school, probably reflecting the poet's idealistic outlook.

The dramatic changes in the political landscape at this time raised hopes of a bourgeois renaissance, and it was in this context that Palamas assumed the role of *national poet*, as the optimistic leader of such renaissance and the "bard" who promoted national ideals. In particular, his two great compositions, *The Flute of the King* and *Twelve Narratives of the Gypsy*, reflected national aspirations for territorial expansion and expressed a call for the triumphant rebirth of Hellenism. Clearly, in the poet's mind at least, this kind of patriotic poetry was tantamount to a political act.

There aren't any translations of this poet's works in the English speaking world and this is the main reason I decided to delve in its translation. This book, which in Hellenic is called *Twelve Narratives of the Gyspy* along with *The King's Flute* are considered his most important poetry books and both consist of twelve long poems named, logos one, two, etc. The word logos means a speech or narrative hence from our choice for title of this edition.

I found Palamas's poetry very difficult in comparison to works of other poets I've translated so far, yet the strong desire to finally present him to poetry lovers around the globe prompted me to continue the effort until I finally came along with a manuscript that I consider excellent approximation to the spirit of this great book: great from a thematic point of view and great for its endless points made about the battle that existed between the conservative poets, lovers of katharevousa, and the lovers and demotic language which represented a modernistic trend that developed in Hellas during Palamas' era and of which he was a good supporter and promoter. I hope readers of this edition will enjoy its beautiful themes and images as much as I have.

Manolis Aligizakis,
apatris, author, poet, translator.

INTRODUCTION

Palamas lived in a socially and politically critical time for Hellas: the era of 1880 – 1900. After the liberation from the Turkish Occupation, Greece had no spiritual people to present except the Phanariotes. There were no cities, only small districts poor and destroyed after the liberation struggle. While schools functioned based on the imposition of the katharevousa*, the effects of ancestor worship contributed a lot to the spiritual conditions of those years.

The scholars of the time, with their puritanism and adherence to patriotism and rusfetology, obstructed the use of the demotic language promoted primarily in the works of Yiannis Psycharis, especially his book "My Journey", which opened new paths for literature. Palamas too did not follow the status quo of his time and became the leader who opened new roads. Knowing the changes that were taking place in Europe and following the economic and intellectual developments on a European level, progressive and free-spirited as he was he conceived the new paths that the literary world of Hellas should follow. In the spiritual rut of his homeland he became a spoiler and a prophet and clashed with the forces which kept his country captive to the old ways and effects. He battled stagnation and opened roads with his prophetic book Twelve Narratives of the Gypsy. He was a revolutionary. A rebel with his verse. They called him dark, nihilist, unapproachable, ascetic, eerie but also philosophical, peaceful and virtuous.

The Twelve Narratives of the Gypsy consists of twelve long poems, each names "Logos 1", 2 etc. The First Narrative is the Coming, (appearance) of the Gypsy, the Coming of the people and of the New Hellenes, of the New Hellenic ethnicity. The Gypsy has set up his tent on the outskirts of Polis**, in Eastern Thrace which doesn't belong to Hellas anymore, a hundred

* Traditional Language
** Constantinople

years before the taking of the Polis. That era is the culmination of the decline of the Byzantine Empire, which is observed at all levels. The people, hungry and impoverished, constituted the helpless mob which the emperors used every time according to their interests. The economic situation was dire, because the Venetians and Genovese had obtained privileges and the monopoly of commerce in the Byzantine Mediterranean. The Church, which played an important role in political and social life, was in decline. "Five hundred thousand well-fed monks, *strong young men* crowded the monasteries, when the Polis fell into the hands of the Sultan". The monasteries and the selected few and powerful people owned 1/3 of the land, legions of the army, the palaces and the monasteries" and didn't pay any taxes.

Palamas in "The Coming" sees Byzantium in decline with all the negative results. The Polis is not a "Guarded by God" but "Cursed by Him". He refers to the history of Byzantium to project corresponding situations of modern times. The City is not Byzantium, but Hellas, impoverished and sold out in 1897 when the Turks almost reached Athens. Palamas cauterizes with his verses the people of the political and social hierarchy that remind us of the Byzantine decline. That time the "Gypsy" like a restless New Hellene, comes and rises above the barren situation of his times to fight for a better tomorrow.

Palamas is not an epic poet in the Twelve Narratives of the Gypsy, he is a true epic poet in the "King's Flute". Here he wants to slander the collapsed Hellas while the *Proto-Gypsy* symbolizes the modern Hellenic ethnicity, he represents the new world that rises and is determined to fight. After all, the beginning of the First Narrative is auspicious as it indicates the era of the renewal, "deep darkness is flooded by a fine whiteness" and it is also worth looking at the environment, which is decorated with chestnut trees, poplars, green branches, rivers and "under nature's main palace, heavens is my only abode"

The Second Narrative is labeled Servant. The Gypsy is about to start his big dream, the renewal of the lands through hard work. But alone he will not achieve anything, he will unite with the people, he will banish egoism: "lean down if you want to rise! Your invincible victory comes when you firstly say, I submit." And Gypsy becomes a copper smith and his first works are chains, nails, keys, shields, swords, beds. But there were no bells for the sheep, nor scythes for the sheaves, no plows. He's not interested in a conventional society. He's disobedient, rebellious, he's undisciplined, he grabs the zurna and he becomes a reveler. But he has other ideals too, he's a builder, a creator, a molder and, breaking his zurna, he begins his work with passion, although they will not let him realize his dreams, they will subjugate his every initiative and he will say: "I experienced a sadness inside me, a huge, insatiable sadness!". It is the sadness of the free man who is deprived of the joy of creation. Disappointed, the Gypsy will look for a new ideal, he will turn to love, which is the Third Narrative, to resurrect the new man, the worker who will be the ruler or the singer and who will rise to become triumphant. But even love will prove to be a liar. The love of the flesh leads to slavery, to fraud, to infidelity, while the love of the soul creates ideals and this true love that creates ideals is missing.

In the Fourth Narrative, entitled The Death of the Gods, Palamas appears to be a nihilist. His gypsy is a destroyer, who destroys everything starting with the Gods. It refers to all places of worship, churches, monasteries, mosques, hermitages, even the Pagodas of Buddhists. He has known everything and rejects everything in order to create a new world. The Ghosts and Shadows of Gods are the false world that must be torn down in order to build the new world from scratch. The Gods are not only the symbols of each religion, they represent all the old values, which must be uprooted to leave free space for the new creation. "I am the prophet, it is I, and I have come to proclaim as king and God the Nothing". Only the word *seduction* recognizes that the prayer means self-concentration, self-criticism. Commentators on the Fourth Narrative have seen Palamas's denial of religion clearly presented in the poem "Tomb", mourning his dead child.

9

The poet in his Fifth Narrative returns to the City, where "the golden and bronze doors creaked and opened wide on their own accord" and the scholars leave the Royal City carrying books and parchments and scrolls and holy relics, as well as Culture and they become citizens of the world. From the shores of Ionia and from Athens the wind carries the wisdom, the word, the rhythm, the immortals and beauty, Plato and Homer, the philosophers, all which will strengthen all nations and grace their youth with wings and will transmit the light of Hellas to the west. The ancient beauty, culture, civilization which were preserved in the monasteries, whatever texts survived the sacred pyre of the monks, remained sterile while they retained certain servility. Palamas does not accept such servility and advocates a new and vital rebirth. *Yet Greece is one, and forever undisturbed. It leaves and you go ahead cry for her!* We could change the title of the Fifth Narrative from the Death of the Ancients, to the Exodus of the Ancients

With the beginning of the Sixth Narrative we find ourselves in a controversy. Patriarch Gennadius anathematizes George Gemistus while Vissarion praises him. Two worlds collide: the world of the ancient Hellenic spirit and the world of Christianity. Georgios Gemistos, philosopher, fanatical Platonist, taught in Mystras the *princes* of the Paleologos. Gemistus wrote the book "Writing Laws" and died in 1452, before the fall of the Polis. Patriarch Gennadios, defender of Orthodoxy fought the doctrines of Gemistos, opposed the union of the Churches and accelerated the fall of the Polis and as a reward for his antithetical policy he was elected by the Sultan as the first Patriarch after the fall of the Byzantine Empire. Around the fire monks burn "the sheets of paper and spirits rise up in the air", while Christians and Gentiles clash. Palamas with this Narrative indicates the eternal struggle between the opposing social forces, the old world that is slowly fading away and the new that is rising. Many modernist, restless spirits of the times wanted to bring progress and reform to education and society but they were criticized and persecuted. Therefore, Palamas doesn't only refer to the pyre of the Byzantines, but his

10

Narratine he relates to the conflict between the Katharevousa and the Demodic usage of language. And here comes the gypsy who is neither Christian nor pagan and believes in the great human values, Justice, Truth, Virtue. He represents the people he met in the mountains of Thrace and Epirus, who have their schools on embrasures and castles and feed on the 1821 songs about bravery. Palamas paid dearly for his preference of the Demodic usage of language as opposed to the katharevousa: he was expelled from the secretariat work he had at the Athens University. But Palamas is a rebel and prophesies the resurrection, although the Gypsy ends his narrative his speech by ringing the "funereal bell"

The apotheosis of the Palamas' exalted creativity is most evident in the following narrative of the Kakava. verse full of imagination, imagery, rhythm, concepts which are displayed in a rich and harmonious way thus constituting the Panigiri of Kakava during which the Gypsies gather in front of Romanos Gate, in a spacious meadow for a three-day revelry, coming from East and West, a custom that served the tax collection policy of Byzantium. Gypsies, gypsies, gypsies, a repetition showing all races, occupations, classes, heterosexuals, infidels, artisans, copper smiths, musicians, hungry and satiated, dreamers and storytellers. The female gypsies also came with wreaths of flowers on their heads. A festival without the participation of women would be half as beautiful and the Greek revolution of 1821 had highlighted many heroic female figures. The King's messenger comes to promise them a home, which marks the autocracy of the era of the first Greek kingdom, and the Leader of the Gypsies shouts "Don't spoil the festival, we celebrate the breaking of the chains." As we delve in this verse, we see clearly the far-sighted insight of Palamas. "and if we fell into an unheard-off fall and tumbled into a crevasse, the deepest of which no tribe has seen before, time will come when we shall equally ascent to the highest, up to heavenly realms." He alludes to the disgraceful loss of 1897 and he prophesies the triumph of 1912-13 war.

The eighth narrative is the Prophetic and it brings us back to the Polis. Outside the Gate of Romanos, the Gypsies Gate the festival of Kakava and inside the Polis is the Circus, the festival of the Byzantines. The nobles, the snobs, the ones of royal descent, the highest priests, the princesses, the queens and the patricians gathered and among them the royal reveller and the master of ceremonies. And the Venetians started their praises and the Greens replied, full of flattering words, while the guards of the east and the guards of the faraway borders were dispersed and abandoned. While the Prophet discerns the nearing black clouds a black hymn broke out, the curse of the guards when the shuddering Prophet shouts "to the chariots, to the chariots! The Turks are upon us" and further down he says: "Karamanitis* is the destroyer of the world and the destruction of nations, the winner of Asia."

The symbolism and metaphor here are obvious. The decline of Byzantine society refers to the faltering, broken society of the times before the shameful outbreak of 1897. Army, administration, education, economy, social welfare, tax policy, all in decay. Greece has become a vast circus and Palamas does not remain unmoved in the face of all these problems and, like a prophet, he has the courage to shout: "Among the praised lands, Praised land, the time will come and you will fall."

The double headed eagle will fly away to the West and to the North. Bitter prophecy and cry of anguish! But the Prophet closes with an encouraging outburst: "As long as God loningly feels sorry for you and a dawn breaks, and redemption calls you, and when you shall not have another step lower, another step deeper on the Ladder of Evil the call will be heard calling you to grow wings again your first big wings of freedom"

The decline of the nation in 1897 was the starting point and was the source of inspiration for the composition of the Twelve Narratives. Palamas, the prophet, envisions the "revolution" that the army and people are preparing for the glorious march

---

* Another name for the Turks

towards the 1912-1913 war, taking into account that the Twelve Narratives of the Gypsy was published in 1907, before the revolution at Goudi took place. Just as in ancient tragedy there are parts which, with their dreamlike descent into the world of mythology, somewhat relax the tragic logos, just as the interlude in the world of Erophili in Cretan poetry relaxes the listener, so does the violin in the Twelve Narratives, which violin works as a sedative tool used in the ninth Narrative. Frustrated by all his searches the Gypsy will discover the Violin of an old hermit, a wonderful discovery. With the violin he will now sing his new ideas and while no one accepted him and everyone chased him away as they considered him unfit, of a different race, a punk, time came when he met the new generation, the children who will shape a new world and the Violin becomes the new way to deal with contemporary issues.

So for the social and political life of the country, Palamas addresses the progressive forces of the nation. With the magical Violin the Gypsy will build the new world in the Tenth Narrative. Out of the three elements, of the Earth, the Sea and the Sky, he will resurrect Love, the Homeland, and the Gods. And while at first he shouted "Hurrah, and again hurrah for every Homeland" now with these three values of Love, Homeland and the Gods, which he had trampled and despised, he will shape the homeland with just laws where the citizens will be free. Palamas envisions Plato's ideal State.

A tale full of elements from Greek and Oriental mythology is the subject of the Eleventh Narrative which is labeled the Tale of Tearless. The course of the Nation and its people is very difficult. They need to make difficult decisions, to tear down everything that stands in their way. The Tearless symbolizes fierce determination and the Smileless symbolizes science, which is the only value, stable and unchanging. Together they will create the new world. The people will offer the crown to the Tearless but he does not accept to be king among the timid and scared people. In the following verse he declares: *I rode on my father//I'm wearing my mother//to quench my thirst// I drank water with Hades*

13

Palamas ends his Twelve Narratives with a hymn to Science and Nature and with an exhortation. Lie down, man, people, lie down and listen to the pulse of the Earth, our Mother Nature. Palamas composes a song for all the trees, the biggest, the proud plane trees, the cedars and for the humblest, the water-loving lotus, and the humble ivy. The first Olympus vanished with the ashes, the second Olympus is the Earth, Nature and the third is Science. The truth lies in Science which deals with life's issues based on science.

The poet Kostis Palamas, the National Poet of Hellas was vindicated. At his funeral, Angelos Sikelianos shouted: "All Greece rests on this coffin".

Georgia Kritikos,
archeologist, philologist

ARRIVAL

The public roads, capes, forests,
rocks are ours. We're arriviste always
moving. Homes and fireplaces are meant
for others.

Ibsen

A gypsy nursed him; for this he has wings

Serbian song

Deep darkness is flooded
by a fine whiteness that
resembles the night: this
was my mind's first dawn

and during the honey-coloured hour
something caressing had
spread softer than
smooth breeze when
it came filled with balsam
of the morning green forests
smoother than soft breeze
and it was in a faraway
land the spring of peoples
and ages: in Thrace.

And there were two opposing
races battling with erotic
mania both yearning to embrace
the most beautiful city

on Bosporus, the only one
both races wanted and dressed
in their shiniest they kissed
the soil their soles stepped on
men fell like grasshoppers
like bees people went there.
And it was the most beautiful
city the between two seas,
an Aphrodite, a fairy, oh
you Constantinople, oh You!
And it was the orchard
of the world onto which, like
a single glory, the people's
poles matched, where unsuitable
barbarians came from
the end of the earth to
the Roman Constantine
to battle it out under
Hellenic banners

and from the narrow
shores of Bosporus
green cities made of sprouts
and fountains rose;
blossoms looked like fairies
flowing, descending
in cisterns: jewels, rain full
of red precious stones.
And the sun reflected onto
the Bithynian mountains
to the Vlaherne and
Magnavre palaces
which unobstructedly rose
and gleamed up high

and from the Golden Gates
to the Heptapyrgion
up to the end of stranded
emerald islands
legions of palaces
and armies of monasteries
as if the spells of witches
were cast upon them and
they spread over the domes
and mansions and you shone
oh my soul over all the motionless
crosses and the cypresses.

In the whitish calm harbours,
double-masted towering ships,
with your lion shaped prows,
slowly rocking upon waves
of what do you dream? Of
which victories and of which
deaths?

And there weren't armies
of warmongering emperors
under the triumphant
banners with eagles
nor were they infantry
nor horse-riding crusaders
that the wind pushed
over hastily
they weren't Arab generals
dragging behind them
Arabian or Turkish army
nor were they devastating
blonde haired pirates;

armadas didn't bring them here
from the frosty north
nor were they from Tauros
nor from Scythia; stirring
the peaceful shores
on dragon resembling crafts
armadas didn't bring them.

And they were from faraway lands
in the darkness of midnight
endlessly walking
day in and day out
as if they had lost their way
and had also slowly lost
their care and concern,
opinion and memory
and every hope, infantry
that left behind a homeland
and won't ever find it
in front of them.

Criers of flutes sighed their
sweetest, secret aches,
ripped and skinned echoes
sounds from tamburines,
horns and zurnas
that wounded people and spread
further out over the white
path and with their rising dust they
fogged the sight of the dark
blue mountain; and heavy loaded
caravans passed. Suddenly
the odd curse, like an animal's
stirring, was heard and

it spoiled the virgin silence
that was spread over the expanse.
Laughter was heard and
you couldn't tell whether
they were of joy or wild frenzy.
Behind the thick blackberry
bushes, lust, insatiable satraps
coupled, you could guess it,
with illicit lovers.

And others,
as of unquenched thirst,
victims of insatiable fairies,
stood by the river's edge
as if forever rooted and
yearning for erotic apexes
with their palms and other
times with their mouths
they bend down to the ground.

And others just out of their sleep
as if tied in their sleep,
you could say they were coupling
wherever they happened to be
onto the barren breast of the earth
or on the softest grass and
they had bulrush branches
laid as beds and
rocks for pillows; and they
were by the river's edge and
in shores and in trenches
as if embalmed bodies
as if undissolved corpses
delivered of their passions

and in their graves; and as if
they were travelling fatherly,
comradely next to
their benefactor Hades
towards the other, silent, life.

Audacious, erected witches
naked demagogues, dressed
like beggars, motionless eyes
like statues, eyes without
glances, which were seeking
hard to decipher oracles, had
gone to the secretive Fates;
cloths of the witches fluttered
imperially in the wind.

And they were stricken by wind
and burnt up by the sun's
conflagration, dwellers
of the desert, ravaged
bodies shuttered by struggles
and struggles, souls untouched
by the lands they had passed
willingly and they were
messengers of a wild spring,
passing black swallows having
curses in their chirps and
contempt in their nests; and
they were all coppery-green
and eternally cursed, loners,
rootless, alien, all connivers
and foreign, embarrassment
of the light, unseen by
daylight while when seen
the day ran to cover its

sunlit face; and they were
gypsies and more gypsies
from afar passing the passes.

Night comes, night returns
just outside of the harbour
night fades in the deep water
fishing lamp made of blood.

It was the time of the steady
thunderbolt, first time ever,
unheard off, from the White
Sea to the Danube up to
the Euphrates delta hanging
over the world, ready to turn it
into eternal scorch and ashes
when the East fainted and
the West shivered like a cane.
It was the days during which
Polis, the harlot, spent her nights
in regret holding her tied hands
waiting for the executioner:
the annihilating executioner.
Russian, Normans, Bulgarians
Catalans, the Christian battling
Saracens, Hungarians the
great horse riders in front of who
all races showed respect as if
to an earthquake.

Polis waited for the Turkish
conqueror.

And times reported of other
worse signs, and there wasn't

any mouth that didn't whisper
about a wise king, about the pale
seer's prophecy of an upcoming
devastation; and it started raining
blood, seven fiery columns
sprouted out of the earth and
a flesh-less hand that waited
for them and unravelled them as
if they were made of yarn.
And fairies and demons
of the night and the underworld
charged to live along with
the people.

And I, amid
the rage and rattle of people,
unaccustomed to a father
and unfamiliar with
a mother, free of all caresses,
stood like a fresh branch of
a not pruned, ageless,
fruitless, deep shaded tree;
barefoot riding a black
stubborn mule, alone tried to
discover who I was (no other
could had ever guessed it) who
covered my essence with a
cloth knitted by the morning dew
and by the hands of rosy dawn.

Oh my black mule you didn't
get any of your father's noble
fate with the dashing body
and from my mother I didn't

accept the scornful serenity,
you said to me, *I'm not the slave
of a slave.* I know it well, oh,
my black mule, you are *you*
you selected two of your
mother's and your father's fate
and you chose your own destiny
and if you aren't as graceful
as the waves nor the bravest
and if you aren't a stooped slave
and a tired maid who awaits
and endures, beauty has turned
you into a thoughtful being; and
if you never said no, you did
because of your stubbornness
not from a peaceful submission.
You're always strong willed
always first always the same
in rivers and in thickets and
on the road and in the noisy
harbours as your steady step
deserves a light, graceful wing;
and if I urge you to descend into
the Tartarus of earth you'll
always obey and I won't even
feel the trembling of your legs;
and if I wake up the longing for
a skyward voyage inside of me
I'll ascend to the stars with you
while your steady steps will
guide me up to that height and
I'll see you as the winged horse
of the magician or the leading
black guerrilla, unbending

barren and stubborn mule.
You and I, both of us, one Fate.
And if I stirred the leaders'
armoury with my hands and
I fluttered the soldier's banner
and my uncontrolled hair
as if I was again commencing
a new battle, as if again
I was ready for long wars
and lance competitions
and wherever I passed along
domed forests of high joined
chestnut trees and hugging
poplars I pushed my mule
gracefully riding on her back
I was the mule-rider who
touched the domed forests
raising my arms and then
going forward or coming back
I always carried leaves and
fresh branches in my hands
and wherever a river stopped
my steps, I disregarded its
powerful current, mule-rider
who I was, I started crossing
in a fastened path that lasted
only while I was passing; and I
was a river passer, a mule rider
an engraving on the rock
mule and man, the same flesh
different from the stone, which
assumed a soul and departed
if I was lost in the deep thought
of struggle, pain and yearning

in my mind the one emperor
having as crown on his head
the crown of the universe.

No homes nor any hamlets
ever stopped you
never blocked your eternal
and unobstructed path,
gypsy, unmatched people
triremes of my land:
behold, untamed mules;
you have tents for sails
look at their palaces and
their temples that are built
in an eye's flash they rise
and tumble as they stand
after they are completed as
your mind creates them here;
and you aren't the gypsy slave
as your home is winged like us
and follows, devoted as it is
to its master and not him to it.
And I the exceptional among
all of you the exceptional:
not a home nor any hamlet
neither a tent controls me
under nature's main palace
heavens is my only abode
and the gap in a tree's trunk
enough to spend my night
the feet of a boulder are always
safe to slow down the run
of my life for a while and
a tumbled house is enough

to spend my sleep dreaming
my most golden-leafed dream,
and a trench deep in the earth,
in which I rest my body and
in which I find freshness and
warmth just to gaze at dawn
with holy carefree eyes and
to sing during the summer noon
like a sweet-voiced cicada.

And I discovered something,
amid the buzz and clatter
of the world, which I grasped
and which had kept me over
the tempest of the people;
it wasn't work of any feather
nor a hand's waving sign
nor was it a castle or any peak
stairway is one and climbing
is another since the heights
existed elsewhere and it was
like the unclear waking up
from a golden dream that
had never stepped on earth
and had its source far away
spreading further and rising
turning into a newborn ghost
like ether amid the ether
thus I existed on a feather's
lightness and height among
the exceptional a special
all my youth and my old age
exceptionally matching with
all seeds and uteri.

THE LABOURER

He truly lived like all others and seemed
to behave like the others yet sometimes he
would strike the drums of logic, sickness
was in his heart not in his mind

Byron

Reality makes me sick and I can't find
the ideals

Amiel

And I dived deep in my soul
as if through the well's mouth
and shouted at my soul
in my mind's voice and
from the depths of the well
as if from long voyages
my voice came back to me.

You're the unique
the incomparable, the special
who's mind rises with you to
great heights: a golden eagle
and your life's concerns
are nothing but games
of the sun with the clouds
like a death that doesn't
kill them when gazing at them
you create, as creator, the worlds.

Incomparable flying game
you are but don't you boast
come close, extend your hand,
help, become a labourer;
match, listen, care and ask
lean down if you want to rise!
Your invincible victory comes
when you say, "firstly you submit!"

Prove that you're the master
you dominate over your anger
your wish, your soul: become
a labourer, erase all of your
personal; place your engagement
ring among the people;
become one with the innumerable
piles of the great comradely
work. Listen to what the tree
tells you, before they cut it
to craft a boat; my eternal soul
lights inside my new body.
The wheat ears undulate serenely
as if they yearn for the last
unborn treasure: bread.
Air, earth, water, fire, of all
the human mind has tamed
nothing has escaped you and
you still hold in your darkness
the untouched and not humbled
and all the vampires of the abyss
and all the morning stars.

The modest horse humbly accepts
its rider, misses nothing and

still assumes its graceful gallop;
the pruning tool hasn't spoiled
the tree with its touch; tree that
feels precious with the weight
of its juicy fruits.

And the mason who holds his
hand and his imagination when
at the request of the priest,
engraves the image of the Lord
in the cradle, the always same
child, he finds place to lay it down
as he finds love in his heart and
bowing before the child he shows
his love for it: thus you love it,
my populace, and you revere.

Thus I became a copper-smith.

The furnish gleams as
the breeze blows in it
the insatiable fire is ready
to consume everything

flame embraces the steel
its echoing roar springs out
of its hungry teeth like
a tamed lion like a sprite

and the immovable anvil
and the fast pounding hammer
commence a thunderous battle
hammer becoming the creator.

Pound the chains, as free
and freer than the caress
of a feather, pound the chains
and the evil steel and pounding
you form the nails that will
crucify the prophet.

And make a nuptial bed, oh,
you who makes the bed of
love using the freest grass and
the nuptial bed and the sickle
that reaps the wheat.

Gypsy, work on the steel, you
who has lived in isolation
in high light-blue places
work on the steel, oh gypsy,
in the fire for the fire
make all the spears,
shields and swords.

The miser's wealth, you, who
have never had of such but
the golden flowers of the plains
the miser's wealth forever
seal deep in the safe's depth
make unbreakable locks;

awake all sweet sounds
bells hanging on the necks
of lambs, make them echo
sweetly, the faraway flocks
on crevasses and on hillsides,
oh mule rider make them
sound sweetly for love's sake;

and let a holy stirring come
out of your hands, you the
never touched by fear
created by a godly ghost
let the thundering bell's
holy stirring to be heard
deep in the ocean's soul.

Oh so futile, oh so futile!

And you, my hand, let down
the steel you hammer, stop
pounding, stop the war you
fought against the anvil
I'm the copper-smith labourer
who wished other things and
other things I create.
I'm the copper-smith whose
hammer doesn't create your
nails, nor your arms, swords,
spears, not even the church bell
nor chains, not locks, not even
bells for the lambs, nor ploughs
to open the earth, not beds for
our homes, not sickles, nor
reigns; I'm the copper-smith
whose hammer only creates
nothing but the beautiful and
useless: such first invented and
unmatched is my art. And
I'm magician of the fire and
I find and from it I steal snakes
and monsters and I form them
even more bizarre in steel.

I'm the pounding hammer
who forms a few unnatural
flowers instead of swords and
I'm the tamer gypsy who makes
circles, shadows, griffins and
spells out of fire, some royal
crowns, ghosts, fairies, mermaids
for ships, for palaces that don't
exist anymore useless, unwanted
and peculiar, sometimes missing
the face, the body and always
missing a name; and what angers
the people who sleep with their
eyes open and all that passersby
expel and all that root in this land
and all that love never woke up
and all that never found any fans.
And I'm the hammering man
who surprises, startles and still
keeps going since all easy work
suited another craftsman though
my breath blows onto my work
something barbarous and new
harder than the hardest granite
and when one expects in his
hands from my hands a creation
steady, motionless and hard
I unwillingly bring to him a soft
soul, a sun ray or a wave's froth.

When I noticed that all who
stood and waited started to leave:
all my brothers and the foreigners
next to me, in front and behind,

who expected something great
of my craftsmanship and when I
knew that I wasn't the unfruitful
tree, I didn't take it to heart nor
did I boast since a new thought
came to me: I throw away
the hammer and the kiln's fire

I turn off, my gypsy bag I grab
and start my procession to other
lands and peoples: let them hear
the new crier.

Idolaters Hellenes and Macedonian
Christians, seamen of the white sea
sailors with true Hellene roots
riders from Malta, Western Europeans,
Crusaders, Venetians, Catalans
Turks, Armenians, Slavs and
Germans, Corsairs from Algiers
cursed Manicheans, soldiers and
frontiersmen, guerrillas from Olympus
all pallikars born in the East and
the West, South and North, Bedouins
from the desert and Arab generals
from the Syrian castles, barons
from Logovardi, Scandinavians,
Russian dignitaries, magistrates
golden eagles of the nobility.

From the forests of Bulgaria
through the oak trees of Thrace
the cedar forests of Taurus and
from the silvery olive tree groves

of Attica and from the yellow
flowered citrus trees, of all
the people's best froth and
from life's leftover cinders
knives of murderers and
snakes of the connivers from
all the gambling halls and
the hard labour, prairies and
tents, insults of country and
cave dwelling wild beasts
from all the brave men on gallows
they all came and stood before me:
the imposing and the unrestrained
and the tough drunk revellers
with warring joy and ardour and

they all cried out and ordered:
make the voice of
your zurna, oh glorious crier
worthy of our celebrations.

Oh long nights and festivities
not the heat of day nor the snow
the daylight or the night
will ever make you stop,

oh night vigils and festivities
how the fields and crevasses
harbours and neighbourhoods
were filled by you,

oh long nights and festivities
how the chorded zurna
encircled you with
a demon's endless roar,

oh night vigils and festivities
how you've dragged me
and how you started and
with song and death you stopped.

Oh long nights and festivities
under the immense starlight
in monasteries and in houses
in long ships and darkest taverns

on the castles that chains
and abysmal ditches besiege
in turrets where noble maidens
abductors of the heart reign

and in the thorny ruins
in the light that gives birth
to the agate's dream
over the peaceful waters

opposite all these and in them
I the ravaged gypsy singer
was a foreigner in all
I always looked from afar.

Around the whirl of passions
I was the serenity
I was the clear breath
amid all the destruction

untouched, flesh-less and godly
oh Paradisiacal desires
and skies of endless lust
has anyone enjoyed you like me?

I still see you around me,
oh lustful and naked
oh sinful buttocks
oh life-suckling embraces,

oh embrace of the prostitute
oh nakedness, oh kisses
oh sobs and moans of the kore
who prostitutes herself!

You've filled my imagination's
four levelled stratum
you've left behind
gleaming, stained marks

all contained and unaltered
in my imagination's four
levelled stratum, in Olympus
and in Tartarus, yet my soul
remains unstained.

When one day I was alone
far from the buzz of the world
by a lake's edge, I the lonely
I with myself I alone
and I gazed at the clear waters

and so deep inside of me
my heart's oh blooming flower
that recalled a softer grief
and unfolded a deeper concern
vague sundown all around
the youngest lass in violet

embrace was putting to sleep
and everything stayed immobile:
the myriad of white lotus,
the tall and swaying cane-fields,
all the flowers and hairy stacks
resembled a picture thin and
colourful that you could see.
They were all totally silent
nature's silence that tuned
its ear to hear the big secret
never been heard before.

Suddenly the devil urges me
to curse the most holy and
the quacking of the gypsy's
zurna, blowing I awakened it
and I slaughtered holy silence
with its great secret that goes
and goes to the shivering lake
all around me and close
the sound charged like a dragon
lusting the virgin nature.
But when I sinned with my mouth
my soul cried deep inside me
oh I the cursed, oh I the sinner
the bloomed flower of my heart
stirred its leaves, stirred
the geraniums to their last
and strong and secret smell
in regret and supplication.
And while the stringed zurna
violated and ruined nature
I leaned my face over the lake
that sorrowfully smiled at me

and I saw the gypsy's face
spoiled and swollen and wide
and wretched and most ugly
that resembled a scarecrow's
having none of its stature
having none of its good air.
I broke the zurna to pieces
and threw them in the street
when they saw me a builder.

Where the huts were before
a palace was erected
by your back and by your hands
reckless, useless gypsy;
Here is the unused, the uncut
marble calling your hands
careless gypsy carry it
to your shop and chisel it
craftsman builder I leaned
my panting chest; new and
from the soft work of my hands
the rough marble took its shape
as I stooped my poor body
to erect a single column
I got to know the heaviest
anguish of matching and
on the airy scaffold I walked
for another kind of a job
I stumbled and I tripled
the vertigo froze me as well.
My hand worked all over
on ebony bed-covers
and crystal partitions, on
forged steel attachments

and all stony tiled floors
decorated to their expanse
by multitude of statues
the big gates and the guards
the gargoyles and mermaids
for all visitors the four-folded
glories, arms and crowns,

the purple columned stoas
there painters resurrected
the ancient and golden battle
of giants; and the wide open
windows with their colourful
frames and shining glasses
adorned the sun rays of fountains
lightning bolts of gleaming eyes;
and all alabaster and enamel
and the four layered walls
(all of them, oh Logos, put on a line).

Made of stone or cedar or steel
each one a single rampart
rooted deep as foundation
each of them knows me well;
yet of all these exquisite pairings
best is the palace by a slave's hand
my hand that has created it though
I know it not nor it knows me.
Oh you unfinished palace
oh estate among estates
I alone crafted you,
all alone all alone I've
incised you inside of me
like a free and soft game

39

in a flash of a thunderbolt
you the most precious of the world
hiding from many people.
Which tireless builder of any race
of my community of workers
oh envy of the mountains
and pride of the plains
on my master's first command
will apply and will raise you
in Eros' world creating wish
and in its superb knowledge?
As if a man's incapable wish
will render you invalid
which great fairies' dance
in the tempest of the seas

and in the roar of the winds
will ever commit to build you
unshakable and in the ages
and ages forever and ever?

(And when they came and
sent me away, builder among
the other builders, and they said:
"gypsy, go, go away" and
when I left and all alone
I took my lonely road
a deep I felt sadness yes,
inside me, a great sadness.)

Third Narrative

LOVE

I'd become diaphanous like dawn
and morning dew, you'd become strong
like the sun and the sea
                    Swinburne *(Triumph of Time)*

Gypsy girl with a partridge's chest
oh, enchantress when you speak
your commanding words
to the stars at each midnight

speaking you become a giant
passing over all the worlds
while the stars adorn you
with their exquisite crown

around my waist wrap
the belt of your manly arms
I'm the wizard of endless love
oh enchantress of the stars

teach my how to read
the Fate of nations and mortals
the apocrypha of the cycles
and the endless of the skies

how in magical mirrors
I might be able to resurrect
the most beautiful maiden
of all the ages and of the worlds

how, following the crafty
words and demons' potions
to wrap them tightly
around the golden rings

as I match words with logos
demons and fairies again
in the golden ring of time
and its rhythm

how with Solomon's seal
I can lock and double lock
all the great spirits
in glassy narrow vessels

and how to throw the glass
in water which will always return
from the abyss of which it is
to the same abyss it belongs.

(Thus like another spirit
the most glorious soul
trapped in the body's
narrow prison glass

in the endless sea of thought
wretched and winged
it lives as in the motherland
an abyss like an abyss too.)

Teach me how to read
secrets of the far and beyond
in the school of your embrace
in the sweetness of your kiss

everything around calls you
omniscient and wise
only one thing you're missing
here, we together, the ONE!

Since I also know I have
something to give you
special as you stand like
an empty pitcher in front

of the deep water that
I'll fill. I know of the holy
music, my violin's tune
you'll enjoy along with me.

The music will take the flesh
of our creating fire
and perfect children
will be born to us

and to more they'll give
birth, while all diseased
or ugly will vanish
from all around them

the law of Joy will shine
of which the king commands:
when you're healthy
you're victorious and strong

and man dwelling in the gleam
of his new and wholesome life
will always become either
a ruler or a free singer.

Oh bird nests oh nightingales
all the unmatched and rough
a motionless rock always
conceals the dead slavery.

When the last born will
slowly come he'll turn into
a more fruitful offspring
with an always deeper meaning

a new nobleman will appear
with his broadsword
that resembles
the most harmonious guitar

and of the unfortunate man
who day after day toils
the disinherited who ends
a slave or a torturer

and whether torturer or slave
the unsaid and the unbearable
he endures the tyrant's
fear remains deep in his heart

and the unfortunate man
will triumphantly rise
prophet of a wide open soul
over the whole of earth

I know nothing of religions
I don't bow to any Gods
you're my acquaintance
my belief, all the temples

I've visited, made bare of
all altars, holy mortal remains
holy crosses and every
sanctified communion

chalices and candles
all the blessings of a heart
I have thrown all these flowers
so you can step on them!

I said and you leaned and listened
oh my alas and thrice alas
to the school of your embrace
with all your fine kisses

gypsy girl with a partridge's heart
oh enchantress as you talk
to the stars at each midnight
tongue with its commands

in your fruitful mature
breasts I discovered
a woman's great deceit
and the slavery of flesh

and the soft and fooling love
and a sickly dimmed light
and the power that wins
over every other body

and I felt deep inside me
something stirring like a feather
which you crashed
with your manly hands

45

oh far away and near me
at midnight when you speak
to the shining stars, to all
with your commanding tongue

and when you tightly hold me
in your erotic and strong arms
oh woman like all others
liar, and slave of who you are!

DEATH OF THE GODS

The Gods have spoken
~Sophocles (Oedipous)

Land, sea, gods meant to perish
~N. American Indian song

You have created all
these temporary ghosts
～Leconde de Lisle

I put up my tent on grounds
I passed opposite temples;
I familiarized with churches
mosques and monasteries
I discussed religion with
Levites and many other believers
in basilicas and morning matins
everywhere from the Hellenic
ruins to the adorned pagoda
I smelled and leafed the many
roses of religiousness.
I remained independent
not a slave of prayer or offering
I'm a prophet of the godless
my life is just a miracle
only once in Constantinople
the saintly desire touched me
it was you who blew it inside me

gypsy with the dishevelled hair
and your crazy running
in three forked streets and
corners, with dogs barking
behind you and the children's
stones following you, mob
with bells they expelled you
oh let be cursed the moment
that gave you birth in which
angry uterus you grew
leftover rubbish of the world
where are you denier of Sibyl?
Your rough voice called it
how can I ever forget it when
you yelled: fire to burn the Paradise
you yelled: water to extinguish Hell.

Grand passages of gods
in whom I don't believe
more grandiose than you
I serenely gaze at you

through thick forests and
wild crevasses this
black, trotting and
unsaddled mule carries me

ferns and wild bulrushes
cypresses and tall spruces
and all other trees in both
sides also gallop next to me

they too fly by like birds
they too behave as if
frightened and scattered
by wild winds and tempests.

Yet despite all your efforts
you don't ever fool my eyes
all you wild winged beasts
nor you birds neither horses

I'm the one who runs not you
you're rooted in the ground
soon as the rider will stop
you too become immobile

grandiose adventures
of the immortal gods
where ever you may exist
oh you shadows of ghosts

all you illusionary giants
oh to all you gods, alas
from the moment a man
will ride a horse before you

and will stand to observe
how you behave like the oak
or like ferns and will notice
you are hanging from his hand

and knowing that you hide
from their view
the airy face of the deep sky
he'll forever separate you

from the sun you hide too
he'll take the fire to light
and warm his humble home
and he'll burn you with it.

No one's birth nor death
will ever block my view
since of all I'm the freest
declarer of the Nothing

I the eraser of the why
I the denier of Something
fly in the air, unsaddled,
oh untamed mule

the curse of thunder and
lightning come from my lips
never was aimed at you
whoever God you are,

I've never felt desire, fear
or momentary anger at you;
who can fight what he can't think
or tremble of what he hasn't lived?

I can delve in your image
as much as I can straddle
my steps over the sea
nor have I begged under

your shadow nor have
I ever knelt before you
nor have I tied myself
trembling under your sky.

And the language I've spoken
and (where, how, when?) I've
learned, and kept it a corpse
dressed in your purple robe

and in the language I've renewed
and have enriched with
a thousand golden words
from the East and the West

only one illusion exists
only one word: prayer!
Oh temples, prophets, idols,
idols, prophets, temples

since I've walked far from you
it appeared over my steps
the saintly potion
the future herb of the world

that sprouted out of my step
the herb that redeems
which flowered in my life
and sprouted in the desert

the herb of resurrection!
When the time will come
that will spread from the desert
to the ever crowded city

that the people will rejoice
cutting its victorious thorns
smelling its auspicious fragrance
when that time will come?

51

Oh the superb fresh fragrance
the loud cry of victory
after the years of slavery
and years of incarcerations!

On the day when man
will bring from the abyss
new virginal roses
like newly created corals

when the sky will transform
from the anguish of its soul
and the fear into an immense
diaphanous light again;

yet if man's fate has it
that forever he'll wait for you,
oh saintly and not hymned herb,
and if he's meant to run

spending his frankincense
before the ghosts of others
and his power in front of
the feet of useless idols,

and if he needs prophets and
crazy for one God declarations
and if he wishes masons and
good workers to create idols

I'm a prophet too and from afar
I have come to declare
the God and King of Nothing
and to the ages ans ages amen!

with no hatred, nor Eros
I, the mason, have come
for your false dreams, oh man
the new temple to build:

the monster statue of Nothing
with all the world's religions
a horrible monster that you'll fear
and at whom you'll also laugh.

DEATH OF THE ANCIENTS

At the moment when the Hellenes were meant to
become slaves of the barbarians and before they
could loose their name and identity they lighted
the almost burnt out flame…yet after their fall
running away from the ruin of their motherland
they became the guardians of Europe

~ Leoparthes

And the three-fold, golden
and bronze doors creaked
as if they groaned and
without any tirade, as if enchanted,
on their own they opened wide

and down below at the shipyards
and the unconquered castles
where deep blue and fresh rubies
scatter rising on the slopes
the waters of Marmara encompass
the craftily built harbours.

And many ships from Europe
galleons from Genoa sail
and Venetian sailing boats
as if waiting for precious cargo
for long voyages and celebrations.

Flags on their masts and
figureheads on their prows
faces from faraway lands and
kingdoms, hearts that beat and
arms extended as if something
to embrace, banners flutter
like kerchiefs.

And from ladders and seashores
of the opposite Asia and
far away from Bithynia
something pitch black spreads
and slowly comes near
the wrath of God and demon's mania.

The waves' song sometimes fades
in the noise over the lands, other
times slowly matches the serene
murmur of the unquiet thunder
and you hear a horse's trot
or the roar of the infantry.

From the wide opened doors
multitude of people come out
slowly dragging their heavy feet
as a litany you don't know for
who it is: welcoming greeting,
goodbye, litany or funeral.

A procession with no flabbela
with no crosses nor any banners
no Gospels nor any priests:
of which religion all these are?

Not accompanied by psalms
nor lighted by any candles.

There are no women nor any children
only old grey-haired, middle aged men
and lads and they slowly come
stooping and tired as if getting out
of hiding places inside the earth or
from some sunless dungeons.

They stop awhile and tremble
unfamiliar as they are
in the road and under such sun
with their hands over their eyes
and their hands on their foreheads
as if blinded by gleam and fear

and they walk away frightened
by the sun light and the far gleaming
sea, by the horizon's edge and
the sky over and around them
as if in a daylight game.

They seem as if they are born to
stoop over hard to read
books and old synaxarions
and over something more precious
than the Arabic topaz and
pearls from Hormuz

as if they sprang up from counting
many practical medicines
in notebooks forever unopened
and as they proceed and

as they come close you can see them
holding something in their hands.

Staffs of pilgrims they hold
and wreaths of criers made of
wild olive tree branches
their roughly nailed sandals echo
hanging off their shoulders
with their travellers' bags.

(And the emancipated waves
rise on the marble quays
splashing endlessly and frothing
and from far away is heard
the horse's gallop and
the coming infantry's roar).

And one next to the other
and two together
and four and more they
tightly hold scrolls and books
in elephantine gold cases

exquisitely engraved and
they walk with all these
and they carry them on shoulders,
underarm and on their chests
as if they are miraculous
icons and mortal remains
and heavy pitchers filled
with ashes of their relatives.
Scrolls and books with faces
resembling purple robes
with satin flesh and painted

in various colours, covered thus
you see them from afar and
believe they are steles and
exhausted altars, flags and
censers and royal crowns.
They look like statues of gods
like glyphs of heroes
visions of prophets and
coffins and graves
offerings they carry
to lay before the feet of idols
and worlds who expect them
and they attend and celebrate
festivities in temples and
faraway places that stand
waiting patiently to get
fully lighted by them.

What are the notes you keep
and all the parchments
reverent flocks where are you
headed like outcasts in the storm?
And in all these books
and these graves, which
diamonds, which wisdom,
who are the dead and
which their holy bones?

Something stirred amid the crowd
a voice like a wave answered me.

Here enclosed in these coffins
in the scrolls are hidden well
(may the nature not cry for them)

oh unspoiled springs of thought
oh unclouded skies of Arts
all the Immortal and the Beautiful.

They are the teachers of truth
believers of the wholesome beauty
old men, pure, forever young
suns given to you to enjoy
in the freshness of an April
the Immortal and the Beautiful.

From the shores of Ionia
and from the air of Athens
which creates pneuma as it likes
from the holy grounds of Hellas
Wisdom, Logos, Rhythm
the Immortal and the Beautiful.

And there is Plato and behind him
heroes of Ideas, the philosophers
I'm with them, Grace says,
and there is Homer and behind him
all the hymnists, Olympian creators
the Immortal and the Beautiful.

They leave their last homeland
exiled by the wind's strong blow
gypsies they become and Hebrews
always homeless, and victorious
they become citizens of the world
the Immortal and the Beautiful.

I know them, I know them
I said too

I know them I declare them
I know of all the songs
which I always arrange
in my own special tune.

And the speech they've started
I finish like this:
the Immortal and the Beautiful
pushed faraway to these lands
by the winds and the rough seas
by earthquakes and destruction
shipwrecked and badly wounded
by their kin and by foreigners.

They've found shelter and skete
monasteries and cells
palaces and schools
but they found no sun
nor freedom
and they got stuck and sick
their Apollonian bodies
got diseased and they turned
into ghosts and vampires.
They met with castles and
hard labour in the temptress
a narrow minded land and
they became stuffed birds
of prey, sorrowful relics
and their lives, young and joyful
they turned into frozen princes.
They either became like
sickly flowers in tropical
hothouses or they sprouted

like ivy surrounding
tumbled ruins. They lived
wrapped in their teachers' hands

and under watchful eyes
they wasted their lives in notes,
they experienced slavery
their tyrannized life and
they met with cursed religion
like torture and contempt
thousands of years and again.

A courageous soul sprang
out of those scrolls and
a triumphant hymn was heard
as if coming from the depths
of their graves:

we shall pass lands and seas
we shall stand where a Turk's .
foot can't step on us, we've been
sent away from our lands
and erased from the East
we shall dawn in the West.

Wherever we may go we
shall find and shall adopt
a new motherland, from
Bosporus to the caressing
Adriatic we shall find refuge
in Venice, roots we shall
spread in Rome and
Florence will embrace us.

We shall straddle over the Alps,
the current of the Rhone we
shall surprise, we shall colour
the darkness of the north
with white, we shall charge
the mind of April and May
we shall sow a new Hellas
and a new youth in every
land we shall grow roots

and wherever we find
darkness we shall spread
new planets shining in
our splendorous light,
ascetics will befriend
life again and you will
again drink the milk of joy,
oh fasting man, a glass
of wine will make you drunk.

The Celts and Goths and
Germans and all barbarians
will rejoice in our company
and first of all the Italian
cassock covered priests and pontiffs
will bow before the feet
of Helen and they will
revere the swan of Eurotas.

We shall teach the mason's
new rhythms and wise laws,
governors and craftsmen will
run to us, towers will be built
and cities and courthouses

of goodness and beauty
will be erected across the lands.

Soon as we resurrect from
this old cemetery into the light
and in the fresh air when we'll
return we'll regain our youth
out of the narrow coffins
Ceasars and Alexanders, with
the power of the sword or
of logos we'll open the new roads.

Peak of Olympus and Parnassus
with our mind and with our arts
the Parthenon and people are created
true resurrection of the soul!

The great Pan will again
be revered into the eons.

And all the mean spirited,
sterile teachers, who have
kept us in such coffins and
walk along with us dragging
the holy leftover corpses
of our plundered race

upon seeing our golden wings
rising above their arms
in an unparalleled apotheosis
they'll believe that like golden
dreams we are reborn and they'll
also shine like demigods in
the splendour of our gleam.

And my soul replied
saying
as if our Immortal and the Beautiful
stood erect before me.

You will pass over
the sea of people like
a breath of soft mistral
that like a wave creates dreams
giving them a lissome
body like the virgin's.

Yet in the sea of people
after you and always
like yesterday, a thousand
winds will be kissing and
battling, a thousand
tempests and snowfalls.

Yet in the sea of people
the month of May which
gave you birth won't return,

since you're passing breeze
eternally undulating blown
by all winds like before.

What if you're immortal?
You lived the true
life only once in your
healthy bodies under the sun
and in the wind of our
miserable motherland;
now you live under a

different sun and in another
wind and you'll never
relive your lives oh, fairies.

Hearts and cities bloomed
and stooped
because of you,
adorers of Hellas before you
shadows and idols
yet Hellas remains intact
please don't cry for her

and each person who'll
become your slave and
alone or as a whole nation
stand against you, he'll
perish with you.
Only the one who won't
loose himself in you
he who adorns his head with
your flowers, only he has
the right to go in front like
a new groom, adorn by
your grace, he'll deserve
to lead us all.

Know it: prosperity isn't for
slaves, let them have a master
whether rich or beautiful;
know it: prosperity is only
meant for free people,
for us.

You'll pass like us gypsies
sowing seeds of free men
and the scorn of any slavery
any slavery with any name
you'll sow thus, because of you,
all the world will come near us.

And if you prefer to be armed
by discipline, health and
decorum, great for you, snow-white
splendorous brothers of ours
your race like ours, won't
settle anywhere.

Let your passing, my white
brothers, be more melodious
than the gypsies; let
all mouths gape open
in awe for you, and let any
hand extend to grab each fake
diamond shining on you;
you will always stay aside
of all nations, even if you
side with them, they will
always stay away from you;
yet with us, oh blessed ones,
all the curses and all the scorn
the world will pass us by
like barbarians and rajahs.

Oh Immortal and oh Beautiful
you might help pave

the path of nations, yet you won't
ever grace nations with wings

and youth; legs and wings and
youth belong to all nations.

Oh Immortal and oh Beautiful
you'll pave the path of nations
like star darkened for long eons
while its light still shines like
an orphan among the infinity
and shines over the night traveller.

I'm not afraid of the Turks
the talons of slavery can't
subdue me
nor the Hellas you propose:
it doesn't touch me,
your frankisence hasn't
overtaken me nor any past
glory, nor any past religion.

Every papyrus I find, I burn
to get light and warmth
I put my fire in every
tumbled deserted building
I find, in a palace or each
monastery, in a school or
in a temple
and from the fire and warmth
all birds and serpents and
trees shine, stretch, shiver
and cry, all nature becomes
a pneuma and whispers in
my ears future spells and words.

Whether music or a gleam
you are the path or

the breath of a lost soul;
oh most beautiful ghosts,

I'm whole, I'm truth
I'm both the inseparable
flesh and soul.

Yet the procession with holy
remains stays silent
it proceeds to the ships
to become invisible yet.

And through the same wide
open gates, before you even
felt it, the horse riding Sultan
the conqueror has entered.

AROUND THE FIRE

*Well, for these reasons, and because he was not a man
of any quality since his ancestral origin was an apostate,
which he became, and because today our nation is in
a horrible state, so not only to make him disappear but
more to punish him we decided to burn his book.*
Patriarch Gennadios *(on the book of Gemistos)*

*Hellas has given birth to many men with excellent virtues,
distinguished in wisdom and grace. But Gemistos excels
as much as the others, as Phaethon differs from the other stars.*
-Vessarion *(epigram on Gemistos)*

Each diaphanous race springs out of a mountain peak
-Leconte de Lisle

Whitish blue dawn shone
while endlessly roaming
I reached a huge gathering;
totally burning countryside
denial of everything green;
wide red shore, a burning fire
men in cassocks all around,
monks, Christians feeding it
stomping the soil rhythmically
in horrific and lustful cries.
And the fire burned black
papers, sheets of papyrus
resembling bodies, hands
and faces amid the smoke

the flames, the sparkles
a few minds flew high up
matching their flight with
the skylarks'.

And further away stood
another group, presenting
noble thoughts and kind
sadness.

And I knew them,
the polytheists, persecutors
of Christians, pagans and
philosophers, dream chasers
kneeling worshippers
of the forgotten Hellas
who observed the fire on
the holy altar as if guarding
remains gathered for
their new temple.

*Watchers of the fire, what
of this fire burning here?*

And they looked at me and
said, "tremble, gypsy and all
you unbelievers. We burn
the cursed, evil book
written by Gemistos*
who doesn't accept the
Virgin Mary nor Christ and
on altars and thrones he
worships demons, ghosts

---

* Neoplatonic Byzantine philosopher, politician

and the pagan idols of
many peoples."

Loud psalms spread over
the sweet and rosy dawn
embroidered by the newly
rising splendorous sun;
psalms of Christians and
psalms of the polytheists
and the Gyspy's psalm
the third and last.

CHRISTIANS

Desolate, enslaved, bitter
Romiosini* I met the curse
of Satan who spread it
like leprosy and famine.
Who can remain tear-less
upon seeing your condition?
For which sins are you punished?
The wise owl withers in your
royal palaces and the wise owl
withers in them. Death's
arrow in the bow of Antichrist.
Desolate, enslaved, bitter
Romiosini arrow pierces your
heart and eliminates you.
Heart, knowledge, mind and
the golden bottle of myrrh,
all these have vanished
you are left with a drop of

---

* Name of Hellenic Nation during the Turkish Occupation

your mother's beliefs and
the golden bottle of myrrh,
all these have vanished
you are left with a drop of
your mother's beliefs and
Christ. Don't let the godless
take away your last treasure.

With the Lord's grace stand up
on your feet, search in your
empty heart for a sparkle, stop
your grief, gather dry wood
from around you and start a fire.
Burn: the atheist's book
inspired by Satan before your pure
and virgin ways fall in its snare.

Desolate, enslaved, bitter
Romiosini they have
blasphemed at you, let it be cursed
before it becomes disease and
wound, and leprosy and fall
upon you like misery. Burn it.
Make ash of it.

POLYTHEISTS

Blessed be, you, who decided
to take upon your shoulders
and rebuild the tumbled
temple of the Hellenes. You
placed the statue of law upon
its head as its coronal, you

incised the logic of Plato
in its marble columns.

You saw the lawless and
endless world of souls and
gods along with masters and
slaves harmoniously and tightly
held together and putting aside
shadowy and smoky idols you
proceeded straight to the cause;
and in a revered hiding place
silently you built your exquisite
Spartan city away from the eyes
of the impious.

Among the half-alive Christians
you rebuilt the new Olympus
and nations of new immortal
stars; Lycurgus and Plato met
in these locals; you rejuvenated
the logos of Zoroaster.

And after you raised your child
you felt tired and leaned, wise
mind, timeless equal to the gods
death slowly took you and you,

blessed one, passed taking
along your wish to dance
your Iacchus with the gods.

Wise judge, prophet, you shared
with us the milk you suckled from
the nipple of heavenly Aphrodite; for

the world you leave your miracle
though the crippled, blind and
jealous, out of anger, throws it
in the flames.

Yet the wind around your flame
becomes a breath of wisdom
and from the flames your mind
rises with great wings and
flies straight to the sun; we
keep your burnt up body, treasure
of your ashes we create.

GYPSY

Hellenes, chasers of Christians
polytheists, leftover relics
selected and accounted, you
followers of the Nazarene
populace guided by priests
shout, burn with light, curse
oh you, all idolaters.

None of you and none other
even the most wisest and
honorable will ever keep
the sunlight bestowed unto
you by its rays.

In the dark depths of the ocean
live some huge cetaceans
beyond the light of day, and
they see while the sun doesn't
touch them, their bodies do
produce their own sun

74

phosphorescence is their foggy sun
that spreads a dreamy gleam
in the dark depths of the ocean
you too live like cetaceans.

Neither the Olympian concepts
nor the names of beautiful
gods honourably inherited
nor Golgotha's crosses
nor the Virgin Athena
nor the Holy Mother of God
nor the icons of holy saints
the miraculous which you revere
nor the most beautiful bodily
statues of heroes and ancient gods
nothing, none of them is useful.

None of you commands
nor dares keep
the wholesome Justice and
unbreakable Grace
since hatred and anger
drag some of you to the left
and others to the right and
the whole land isn't enough
and if they gave you the whole
planet each of you would try
to keep it to himself.

Light the fires oh monk
burn, burn what you burn
is all in vain; from the ashes
of your fire the golden eagle
of the mind rises and spreads
its wide wings high up

toward the light
and you oh philosopher, create
the polytheistic religion,
take names from the ancients
the mysteries of the Chaldean
all your creations, in vain!

All you build is but a grave
all white, grand and solemn
and what shivers slowly over it
just the shadow of a tree
of that of a vampire.

Neither Sparta, nor Athens
not even the Great Polis.
Athens got poisoned by
a Hebrew woman from
the midst of Gethsemane.
Where is Sparta? I know
nothing of it. I know
Mystras. And the world
famous Polis under the Turks.

Yet from all this death, all
this enslavement and pain
slowly, tenderly and longingly
new catharsis and new life
spreads over all lands
from proud mountain peaks
to all the tender shores.
Where you'll find a lone footprint,
oh monk, that reminds you
of the Olympus, a soft Siren
song if you ever hear

you condemn it to Hell
and if a tender lily springs
out of the ancient ruins, even
that you uproot and you discard.

Yet all you discard and curse,
butterflies and little birds
with all tender winds, they're
all embraced and transported to
the foreign lands where they'll
become nestles, and sprouts
and fresh flowers.

And a light from the East pierced
the darkness of the West
where flesh, madness and
unobstructed lust spread.
Helicon and Hymettus send
all their light and all crucified
resemble Apollo while Christ
holds up the Orpheus Lyre.

And you rebel chaser of Christians
why you fight with such envy
to return the joyous religion
and you curse and hate all things
while you chant ancient rhythms
your ancient gods and books?
Your struggle is all in vain.
These are different times, different
language, different names and
remember the Nazarene was
unjustly crucified like a thief
and like a killer; his heavy
shadow passed over the whole

earth and the eyes of Virgin
Mary nailed you on your spot.

Time will come when you both,
Pagans and Galileans, will shake
hands, oh you, wide eyed and
drenched by life's potion
you'll see ghosts as ghosts
and you'll extend your hands
to grasp all that have survived.

I revere your flesh-less dream,
oh philosopher, and I build an
altar for it, fresh wind has
blown unto you; I feel for you
too, oh monk, it's not your fault
that you received your duty
from a not smiling, merciless God.

Yet all your holy and honourable
things and what of the others' you
don't recognize I found them
matching, firstly created and
ready to unfold when once I
was a hunter and an anchorite
on snow-capped high mountains.

Sorrowful, tired, overburdened
like a shipwreck, I walked away
to live among the beasts and
I rode my mule to edges and
my tent I put up on top of hills
and in front of deep crevasses and

I walked on the Thracian mountains
and on Epirus' mountain peaks
and I satiated my devouring hunger
and I found a novice populace
travelling away from slavery
along mountain sides and riverbeds
populace unrestrained who knew
nothing of books, who have none
of the statues of the polytheists
who keep schools up on hilltops
and show strength, and desire
for knowledge; people who live
their songs people who resemble
statues of Gods, residents of

the plains fear them and call them
strange names: klephts, border men
and traitors, tyrants and royals hate
them and they are brave among
the bowed and soldiers among
the asleep wearing black scarves
over their heads, call them monks
if you wish, call them philosophers
with their overcoats, call them
pagan; nature's precious they are

call them Christians, followers of
the Nazarene who is full of
youth among them.

All you fight to gain using cheap
ardour of logic they too demand
with their arms and they don't
bend to build vacant altars and

they are fathers of children, mates
of the sun who will establish
their new kingdoms.

They matched the sacrificial milk
and blood with theirs and a
brave heart pulses in their
hairy chests
witnessing, battling, singing
of life and of the crystal truth
come and fight; you'll all pass
fast: alive-dead, polytheists,
Christians worshippers of idols
fragrant mountain air will blow
from the slopes and wild bulrush
and all the shivering candles will
blow out.

And thus I, the smiling anchorite,
the destroyer who blasphemes
in the sulphuric heat of our lands,
feel the freshness of belief inside
of me and I dreamed of living
among them though even them
cried out: go gypsy, go.

Let them exile me. I revere them
I the speaker of beautiful truth
none of the demagogue revenge
guides me and for this I stand
before you so you can hear me
chiming my slow, funereal bell.

THE FESTIVAL OF KAKAVA*

Free verse speaks of free speech
      ~ Andreas Laskaratos

March on! I want the rosy horizon as motherland.
I'm jealous and have a passing sun ray for
my precious fireplace.
      ~ M. Guyau

The wide open field, unruffled
and full of flowers spreads
outside the Gate of Romanus
softly encircled by
the spring orchards; the triple-
double foundation castle,
grand and gracefully standing,
has flowered too, embraced
by ivy, laurel and shrubbery
its warring embrasures turned
into a glorious garden
towards the end of April.

Flocks of animals graze on
the plain, sheep, horses, cows
and multitude of people, who
sometimes buzz ready to
start festivities or war.

---

* Celebration of the cauldron

And now that May has come
with its joyous daughter
the First of May celebration
when the gypsy populace
get drunk, yell and turn wild

over the flowered fresh plain
the Festival of Kakava while
the riverbed that splits it in two
small brotherly pastures that
eye each other across
the mother river, a field over
which a strange celebration
commences, once a year
on the First of May with its
flowers and abundant joy.

The gypsies come and come again
the gypsies who once held
the desire to lean down under
the shade of their tents and
to think they are sheltered in
the warmth coming from a
fireplace and enjoy through
the closed door the freshness
of the forest coming in
through the open window.
And rootless gypsies came
who lost it all, who imagined
they too spread roots and made
relative of the foreigners and
considered themselves equal
to aliens though the foreigners
didn't love them and their kin

denied them: their kin who
hated them more than any other
and all the gypsies came, the
scorned of the most scorned
and their tents were the most
lonely and they were most
ruined among the most ruined

since their home sends them
away and the roads don't
even desire them because
the Goddess Freedom, that rules
over everyone and makes grace
out of evil, deserted them and
they can't live in foul air nor
in the country nor in the city.
Bastards, liars, thieves and
seducers whose evil has no
fire nor air, nor stature
as if they were Christians,
Turks, godless who live here
and there and they're tossed
around, travelling gypsies or
domesticated.

Behold the gypsies, last remnants
of a dead nobility, different
than the raggedly dressed crowd,
with faces glowing in the sunlight
sharp like sharpened blades and
from their unbending bodies
by chance glances, stirrings
still know how to order
still know how to guide.

With hats cover their thick
hairs shading it and flowing
breeze softly stirs locks which
shine like wool shirts or
gold embroidered vests; erect
on their horses, polite captains
with foreheads gleaming like
gravestones, and having youth,
greatness, lives, fortunes buried
in them; and you could discern
on their faces something
eclectic and diaphanous that

before it sinks in the rough sea
stirs on top as if a bitter, last
moment emphasizing their
futile fight for the salvation
that will never come.

And all the well read gypsies came,
the thoughtful devotees who
delve in the explanation of
the inexplicable, the punished
by the endless studies gypsies
came, the seers and astrologers
the shamans and the exorcists
those who explained the dreams
and those came who never stop
narrating their strange tales,
like myrrh and precious stones,
brought from their motherlands
where giants live, the untouched
plentiful lands of freedom and
those who narrate some dark

sorrowful stories, let them be
lighted by the conflagrating sun.

And gypsies came who know
the workings of all planets,
the secret paths of all the stars
gypsies who observe them and
foresee loves, fates, Hades and lives.
The gypsies came who tame
the seven headed snakes
which can kill in thousands
the gypsies came with
their dancing snakes and
using hooks and rings they
hug their snakes tightly.
Gypsies with the Sybil eyes
came and read their women's
eyes and secrets written on palms,
hands, books and notebooks.

Wise gypsies and magicians
they could spread roots anywhere
they wished to look alike any
race they could subjugate
any heart and any opinion, yet
they didn't want anything but
to pass proudly and persistently
strangers among strangers, naked
cursed resembling crows, clouds
and the untiring cranes; they're
gypsies the most capable.

And gypsies came who built
their lives like their houses

founded on horse carriages
rolling along and pulled by cows that
have something of the elephants
and of the travelling ships and
as they groan and echo passing
over rough paths and streets
when suddenly houses stop
with the panting gypsies close
behind they resemble as
something holy and great
like Epitaphios or the Holy Arc.

Here are the Turkish gypsies
who sleep in tents, the pure
race. They always travel in
plains and in deserts the ones
with their invincible souls
their straight and erect bodies
and the wildness of their souls
shines in their lighted eyes
the soft and the powerful as
if made of steel and sting;
they're joyous in the snow
and in the rain, in the sunshine

they celebrate the best festival
on bare earth as Hades finds
the man naked and chokes him
to death in the ripped tent whipped
by the wind that charges and
wilts men as if they're flowers.

Scruffy men, Netotsi,
Gantzay, Roma, Cinties,

Zaparads * all names and
all races and from Bulgaria
from the Danube and gypsies from
Moldavia, Cyprus and from
Caucasus and gypsies from
the Dodecanese**; dark skinned
with bears and monkeys singers
and with curly hair they've all
come, the bums and killers,
religious fanatics followers of
every faith, impious and also
the non-believers, atheists and
those who know how to slip
away from everything though
they remain under the lowest
of the low. And the ones who
live in caves with the wolves and
in burrows, wild men, half naked,
conniving loners having hands
like harpoons and teeth like
talons and they eat cat meat
and meat of dogs and rodents
they do as the condors and
above all they are free and
come out of their caves and
their burrows and here

come the basket makers
and horse traders, farriers,
lumberjacks, farm labourers,
unemployed gypsies and hard

---

* Names of gyspsy races
** Group of twelve Hellenic islands in the SE Aegean

workers who reap the gold
though never seek it and
those who observe it all: the
anguish of work and the concern
friendships and disagreements
the sweat of the family man
and the wife's faint blushing
from the heat of their fireplace
the smoke that spreads over
the house, nobility and poverty
and everything else; nothing
surprises them as they see it all
as in a dream each night under
their tents where they return
being always the same gypsies.

And gypsies came who work
the metal and the welding
the master craftsmen gypsies
and the hammerers are here
with their primeval tools, with
their double bellows, copper smiths
with a myriad tools, specialists
of the always burning pyre
from which they draw all their
strength and power.

And there came the instrument
makers with their music creations
the full of rhythm like a dream
the singing gypsies came who
even forget their language
from one to the other country

that they traverse they change
their language too like their
staffs which they cut from
one or the other tree, their
language changes and as
they steal a few words from
each race they visit they add
them to their words like they
match the horses of their
carriages, which horses they
steal too whenever they
have the opportunity. Yet one
thing they never change: the
fatal result of their gypsy heart
and the soulless creation of
sound, of rhythm and dream
you're their own language, their
only one their secret. The musical
gypsies have come.

And here came female gypsies
wearing celebratory, colourful
dresses off which they had hung
colourful, big, shiny beads,
female gypsies with their red
dresses came and with their
yellow scarves, oh lustful eyes
oh, bosoms, oh lips! And they
came crowned with flowers,
tambourines and belts which
they play as they dance creating
circles and singing of May
and among them one appears
the special one, an eighteen year

old who swings and bends and
dances ready to fly in the air
a maniac's dance from the queen
of dance with the lustful body

the young enticing gypsy
the girl the great enchantress.

Female gypsies came who
sing: here comes May and
the spring, here the summer
comes when the foreigner
wanting to return to his land
puts the saddle on his horse
the golden horseshoes with
the silver nails and you oh
cursed gypsies who don't
have a motherland, no land
awaits for you, only this month
of May awaits for you, the
emperor May is calling you;
come gypsies from the West
and gypsies from the East
the month of May the festive
calls you to the three day
festival to the festival
of gypsy life. And from
the Kakava boiling legumes,
bitter, and harsh, and sickly
food, a little water from
the spring, bring some honey
and some milk, mix them with
water, and bring some old and
strong wine, oh gypsies, oh

magicians, oh wise men who
know well the demons and the spells
from the book of magic.
Prepare your horses in the night
put on the saddles and getting
silver from the moon and gold
from all the satyrs come to
the festival oh, festival goers.

Come join with all the others,
lovers and couples come and
enjoy the three day festival
on the wide open plain find
your ephemeral motherland.

Suddenly on the third day he
appeared on golden saddled
horse the messenger of
the Byzantine king declaring

oh farmers and oh writers and
guards encircle him
the drums echo, the horns
are heard.

Suddenly the unexpected
tidings traversed over
the vast plains from end to end
and spread the deadly silence

and among all the silence and
from above a high terrace
the voice of the messenger
was heard clearly:

Gypsies, the God protected
king declares this is the end
of your endless wandering
and homelessness.

The five caped Taygetus
awaits for you, the mountain
with its shining bottomless
crevasses and Malevos' red soil
the vacant Lacedaemon awaits
for you to occupy it;

its rough plains and
the glens await for you
the heart of Peloponese throbs
for you oh gypsy people.

Go there and build castles
it's the king's command
find refuge in the bosom
of a motherland and
in the shade of a nest and

when you yearn for the clamour
and destruction of war
arm yourself with your hammer
and come under the king's banner
and you too fight heroically.

So you'll have among
the oleanders of Eurotas
your violin's enchanting
echo which will accompany
your magical sauntering and

your new youth shall have
above it the guarding power
of the five peaked mountain
with its cypresses and its snow
with its gorges and fragrant air
and it'll govern over you like
the king's bright forehead.

Yet the words hadn't finished
and I started to talk and
from atop another terrace I
spoke to my brethren.

The anger inside me is like
a volcano and my mind like
the sea; the world of my past
dreams and my future visions

that seasoned our secret world
can't be kept silent inside me.

People of the gypsies listen to me:
I'm the first sign of the new
world that is coming after many
years and I am the one who
lives for one thousand others.
Gypsies, no prophet ever talked
to you with a tongue like mine.

Who's the man who builds
royal castles up in the air and
gifts them to us who's he who
proposes hopeless hope before
our eyes? We're the homeless

93

and the uncured, wail to all
motherlands, wail!

We're the immortal and uncivilized
the cities are dens of serpents
and refuges of all the cowards
of fighting and self-defeat, dens of
wolves, dogs, sheep and shepherds
wail and wail again at their homeland!

Fences are always our enemies
when they enclose the world
wild verdure and nettles sprout
behind them, misery in their shade;
the traitor's conniving wilts all
the mindful ideals and shuts all
nightingales of the heart.

The sin always dwells like a scorpion
inside of them, never the brave lion;
the fence marks the evil man and
the good is but a baby in opium;

work the earth again in your gallows
rejuvenate its good and sins
pounding it with your hammer on the anvil;

Pass over fences, give to your
mules wings and ride them like witches
the world is whole and endless
where the lands end the seas begin.

From atop of each mountain that
you'll climb you'll gaze at other
higher mountain peak, a

different, mind boggling world
and when you'll reach the highest
of the highest peaks you'll still
understand that you live under
the same stars.

The law that isn't given from
the lips of the wise man as god
sent gift, it chokes like a wind
that governs everything, though
we have inside of us the true law
the open eyed law that leads us
each day and night on our wandering.

Who are you who want to nail us
and make us incapable of enjoying
the sun the way we enjoy it now?
Our cup is always full and our
homeland is anywhere the sun rays
reach.

We spread roots in the lands of
the seven rivers where monsters
live and darkness and light too
and man alone stands in the middle
living his life that is burdened
by the ghostly haunted glen.

We've grown amid the swans and
lotus flowers, onto the endless
plains we galloped along with
the beasts next to the mighty Ganges
we loved the gigantic elephants

our ancestors are snakes and
orangutans.

We the race of the bronze and iron,
taught by the hand of the first ever
gypsy father of man, the Cain's
descendants though Cain's curse
applied to us too and drenched our
roots with secret, undissolved poison.

We have never bowed and we never
kissed the feet of the powerful who
stepped on us as if we were worms
our souls defended us with swords
our souls the wisest and dreamy.

We've been humbled and we've
been humiliated in our decisive
peace of hopelessness we've drunk
all misery and horror in this land
where pour lives have rooted,
though we gave wings to our roots
and left far away to openness with
its endless roads.

We left with the swiftness of wild
cats and with the bat's wild flight
with the speed of grasshoppers and
with the disdain that homes and
nests and castles deserve.
Wail and wail to all motherlands.

We passed from India to Iran
and ancient Taurus noticed us when

we follow the path of wandering
merchants and we endured
the misery and pain of climbing
high mountains and passing tundras
glens and rivers, the snow, the north
winds and sandstorms.

In the sand dunes of Misiri* we
left our deep footprints, the Sphinx
was surprised to see us the more
riddled than its face; we shone
from the Nile to Euphrates and
from Varanasi to Aleppo.

And from the castle of Trapezus
on the Black Sea we traversed up
to the great Danube, the Balkans;
our ships moored at Constantinople
the Thracean plains welcomed us
the first wind-whipped caravans;

and if you told us that we'd return
to our lively starting point that
has no borders and all are mixed
up in it, the mountains, verdure,
all gigantic and tied together by
certain magical powers, your
first motherland awaits for you
to give you an unexpected glory
that bestowed unto wise men, and

---

* Egypt

heroes, oh tent people, it will set
the throne of Maharaja for you
and it'll place in front of you, the
lotus flowers adorned along with
all the holy prophets and ascetics.

We'd then shout at you: we don't
want you to ruin our festival; we
celebrate the breaking of the chains
of whatever kind, of diamonds or
gold; we're the delivered ones.
Wail and wail to all motherlands!

And if we have tumbled down
to depths unknown that no other
race ever descended time will
come when we'll ascend to
immeasurable heights onto
the gleaming heavens; we're

the race who are meant to erase
the concept of a motherland,
the precious maya of Brahman
the race of which hands weave the joy
of gods and mortals, its miracle
its best surprising deed.

The whole world is a gypsy,
that sits on a throne and using
his hammer and violin, creates
the flawless Ideal; universe turns
into an orchard and a May festival
for our only motherland: earth.

People will choose a new Atlas
or one Athos* onto which an
expert artist will create our statue
and time will come when a new
star will shine from the depths of
heavens and the world will recite
our names into the ages and ages.

And they heard from both orators;
they found the first one indifferent
and they were surprised by the second
as if they felt something, as if
they didn't understand anything
only they felt as if starting a new
struggle as we do when we awake
trying to catch the dream we saw
in our sleep, which always
touches one and then it always
escapes him.

And as when the wind subsides
and the forest regains its peace
the clouds, which waited to drench
the forest with rain, open up,
thus when both orators stopped
their opposing messages of
the royal messenger and mine
the noisy, thoughtless, festival
recommenced in the Mayan
sunshine, the Kakava festival,
the gypsies' celebration.

---

* Mount Athos is a mountain and peninsula in northeastern Greece and an im-portant centre of Eastern Orthodox monasticism. It is governed as an autonomous place within the Hellenic Republic. Mount Athos is home to 20 monasteries un-der the direct jurisdiction of the Ecumenical Patriarch of Constantinople

PROPHECY

After these events contemptuous and unknown
men governed, both men and women, sinful and
profane…
    ~ Prophecy of Emperor Leo 6th the Wise

Life of a forever young thought sprung out of
his eye, life that pierced through the present, past,
and future.
                                    Shelley

The prophet who stares into
the eyes of a vision,
the prophet who orates from
within the mouth of the future
urged by a breath I don't
know, he's a breath too,
leaving behind all his lions,
apocrypha books and eagles
and leaving them, alone he
went down among the people
in the immense, made of marble,
Circus where the fans were ready
to celebrate the May festival
and all the sinful citizens of
the big city buzzed
and overflowed
the Virgin Mary temple.
And the prophet saw all
buildings and miracles,

monsters born in the kisses
of the sinful and contemptuous.
And he saw the exquisite
idols stolen by barbarians from
places lost in the faraway time.

Idols that fill the palaces
and surprised by their high
columns, turrets, gods and
people, thousands of lives
made of copper and marble
having the elephant's grace,
the value of precious gold
and like anything powerful
and tangible, foreign, standing
and artistic made wisely
an enigmatic artistic creation.

And he saw the rich nobles
heavy and pompous as if
chained and placed properly
around the regal throne of
by the grace of god despot and
he saw magistrates and
lawmakers with golden
bracelets dressed in heavy
cloaks and purple robes
the palace's first nobles
and the adorned with gold
masters of the court and maidens
and princesses dressed in white
who shone like vague stars
and he saw the club-bearing
guards and further out at

the corner he saw the riders
standing next to their horses
with the shining heads and
the Venetian lances onto
which the young fighters
leaned their gigantic bodies.
And the frontiersmen stood
there too, scattered and alone
tired and discarded valiants
and the prophet shivered.

And he never noticed the face
of the Regal leader who appeared
from behind the eagle adorned
main gate of the Palace. He
saw him with the midgets and
the mimes and the circus clowns
and the performers and with
the heroes of the circus.
The King is brother to all
he fights next to them
he drinks and revels with them
in this great immense Circus
which celebrates the May
festival. And he saw him
on the chariot, dressed in
Venetian attire and in the cloths
of the Green charioteers he
stood ready to march and
the prophet shivered.

And he saw the charioteers
dressed in green and those
dressed in blue and he saw

the dog who knew to bark
to obey and to lick and to rage
and tear up, the dog trained
in obedience and trickery.
And he saw the grounds, steps,
roads and arenas filled with
people, dressed in black
woollen shirts, men with short
hair and velvet wreaths and
rosy necklaces and strange
songs and flowers and scarves
in their hands. And innumerable
spears and shields that stirred
and they all, people and officials

waited to start rejoicing in
the spring festival of this
immense circus. And from
the upper parts of the circus
he gazed at the faraway sea
with its sweet shores and
its safe coves, its beautiful
islands in the May morning
the holy sea as if in a dream,
Aphrodite of the shores, the
Sea of Marmara, and
the Prophet shivered.

And he saw the phosphorescent
tower where the guard stood
gazing at the before him expanse
outside the great holy Palace
and the prophet shivered when
he saw the burning flames

which stirred and rose much
like the sun, though flames with
black tongues that spoke and
warned that the Hellenic soil
was trampled and the enemy
was marching against the Polis
the primeval enemy the follower
of Muhammad, the Lord's
anger is the curse of the Hellenes.
To the Arms, to the Arms.
The Turk!

And the prophet heard the tidings
about the coming war and
cried: Lord, my King, all
the messaging fires were lighted
from the peaks of the Olympus
up to here at the Golden Polis
at the hilltop of St. Axentios

to the phosphorescent tower
of the Great Palace! The enemy
is here trampling the lands. We
wait for your command. Stop
the festival, close the circus
place the arms on the royal
Gate of Chalke: sword, shield,
straps, Lord give your order:
to war, my Lord, to war!
To the Arms, to the Arms!
The Turk.

And suddenly the royal king
answered: law giver stop.

Nothing can stop my ardour
nor my joy, nor my festival.

I want to carry as I started
to run victorious to the end
who can cut the golden thread
of my ardour, my joy, my festival?

Not the Turk nor any demon will
stop me nor war, not even an
earthquake, this the plain that fights
for my ardour, joy, and festival.

The horses dig the soil and chariots
wane as if alive and
my people await to crown
my festival, my ardour and joy.

Put out all the fires of war
shut all gleaming lighthouses
tumble all phosphorescent towers
leave my joy, ardour and celebration.

March oh you chariots and charioteers
prepare the sweet wine and
people hymn celebratory hymns
of my celebration, joy and ardour.

And the gleaming fires were put out
all the towers were tumbled
the Circus echoed loud cries
the chariots started their run
with the royal king up front
crowned with rosy colours

in front of the all alone monarch
and the Prophet heard the joyous
hymn as it spread all over
from the mouths of
the Greens and the Venetians.

THE GREENS AND THE VENETIANS

Look at the spring which dawns
again with its rose colours;
it brings joy and health and
happiness to the world and
the Lord sent valour bestowed
unto your king, oh Romiosini!

The East is filled by your image
the West is full of it too
the Danube overjoys and the Kydnos
River longs for you; and I
know you because of your logos
and your fame but don't be
unjust stop awhile and let me
enjoy your face and beauty.

You who have no enemies
wait for me, the barbarians of
the West are your slaves and
all the nations of the east.

Let me wash your feet and
cleanse your hands
let me bath your body and
your legs look exquisite

your hands are bloodied and
your flesh has suffered for me.

I'm pretty and I reign over
all the lands, you're beautiful
as you stand over all nations.
Come let our beauties join and
let us enjoy each other's company.
Over the whole universe
you won't ever find a Polis
to look and shine as I do.
You named your New Rome
over all the benevolent seas
you bathed me with wreaths
of glory you satiated me with
luxuries, crowns and victories
that you placed over my head.
The Scythian and Persian kings
bend down and bow before me.

Take off your iron shirt and
all the arms of battle, put on
what suits you the victor:
the rosy chiton with the satin
flowers and diamonds; come
dismount your horse, so it
too can rest and grace the Polis
with your light, oh Sun King,
spread your light equally
so we won't be blinded by it.

Soon as the hymn from the
Venetians ended a new hymn
started coming from a faraway

corner, a black hymn that
swelled like a wave, the tempest's
offspring and it wasn't hymn but
a wailing and a curse, which
the Frontiersmen sang. When
the Prophet heard it he shivered.

FRONTIERSMEN

Having no ears and no eyes
oh you bony populace,
close your praising mouths
and stop jumping from joy.

A wild drunkenness drags
everything to theatres and
taverns the palatial Polis
and the King.

And they mix with the reigns
of the horse of the crowned
charioteer, the precious and holy.
The African men have arrived!

The Turks destroyers of
the world surround us
the destroyers of nations
the Asian conquerors.

And we the frontiers men
with our silver-made spears
the golden saddled horses
have been utterly discarded.

All the pyres of the frontiers men
were put out from the seas
to the islands all along
the narrows and mountain tops

they were put out one after
the other: pyres, guards and
messengers, dragons war
criers, sleepless lighthouses

and the hands are sitting idle
all the eyes have been shut
the last pyre was put out
by your command oh great king!

The victorious emperors
the flying Tzimiskes and
the killers of centaurs and of
the Bulgarians vanished

and behold timid masters
female, lazy and slow,
great revellers of the circus
gay shepherds of the temples.

The avengers of the war that
just commenced, saviours of
the lands don't ever exist
hanging on the Chalke Gate

they don't exist as before,
the shining thunderous arms
sword, shield, and armour plating
the King's great weapons.

And all around the Euphrates
alas, the crown of bravery
the courageous head,
the rose of Cappadocia

the great man of two races,
the frontiersman, on the open
and in secret killed by Hades
the Romiosisni's great heart.

He's gone, the one you, oh
Romiosini had on the throne
higher than all palaces the king
of kings higher than all kings

the Tower raised on top of
Euphrates is tumbled
the crown of Romiosini and
the reverent moon glow.

The Square Tower with
its eight corners is tumbled
Tower with embrasures
Tower full of windows

that was aimed at Babylon
that was gazing at Syria
Tower with snow that couldn't
melt by the faraway light.

Tauris, Antitauris and Libanese
bowed in front of it and
the Caliphs of Baghdad and
Tarcea with its castles

and we your frontiersmen
tempests of your anger
strange and undue decorations
of this corrupt unsuitable festival

and we his frontiermen's
frontiersmen unjustly dragged
along, oh what a shame, guards
of the gates of unworthy king
like the enemy's avengers

jokes and laughter of the children;
where are you ravines and rivers
hiding places and charging spots
caves, borders and mountain peaks?

The last lighthouse is gone
lights and eyes have turned blind,
the night has spread. Cursed!
The Turks, the Turks are coming!

THE PROPHET

From the extolled lands, you
the most praised, time will come
when you'll fall and your Fame
will trumpet its latest call
to the north and to the south
to the East and the west.

Time will come when
your glory and fame will
vanish; your path just like

the sun's will fade away in
the East and in the West in
the North and in the South;
you'll tumble as the sun won't
ever shine for you again.

You'll get ravaged like the plains
witches have put spells on
your passing which will be as light
as the dripping morning dew
the mourning doves will mourn
for you each evening and the softly
leaning oaks by the cemetery.

The charge of your enemies was
stunned by the miracle of
your fire and East and West
fought against each other in
your castles. And you kept away
all battle deluge and erected
you stood as your powerful peninsula.
They all bowed before you: Turks,
Europeans, and Slavs. You've burnt
all enemies in your fire for eons
and what a Fate, now you'll burn
in your own fire, most unfortunate
alone you'll burn, all alone
you the most hopeless of life.

And they will start a dance
around you, playing drums and
violins, the gypsies and the Jews,
Arabs, and Pashas and your brave
defenders will kneel becoming

slaves of the slaves and your
male youths will be violated
in the embrace of the sultan, beggars
will defile all your remains.

Cursed country from the heights
to the depths, you sinful land!
None will ever lean to give
you the last kiss of death.

And your fall will reverberate
your mourning will be heard
before it will be smothered
by the whole crying universe.

A new world will appear as
if from your ashes, denier
of all your power and glory
the world will talk badly of you.
A World different than yours
one you have nourished with
your milk will pass over your
lands and a spring will flow
out of each step it'll take.

And your Soul, oh Polis,
damned sinful as it is and
dead will leave you and
shall wander searching for
a new generation as if sold out
to demons it will cry and
wander in the darkness like
a shadow in the void, like
a craft in the wild abyss

then the shadow will take flesh
and then the craft will arrive
into the wind-whipped harbour
and you'll still be alive in
lands and time forgotten and
in the history of nations in
the cycles of eons you'll mourn
of your decadence, and your Soul,
like a cursed Polis, won't ever
find a peaceful place to rest.

In the evil body it will forever
reside and step by step it'll
descend life's stairs from an
evil body to another amen.

And a day will come, the
dark day when your Soul, oh
Polis will settle far away
onto the graceful lands lit
by the sun rays, in the April
air and startling the sun
your KINGDOM, nourished
by your shed blood, will appear
in the startled sunlight, like
laughter, a lie, a vague image.

Here's your two-headed eagle! It
flew away, far away with all
your holiness to adorn other
lands, mountain peaks and other
hillsides. It takes along your
crown to the North and to
the West where it establishes

its power, its glory held in its
talons; the laughter and the lie
of the kingdom that was created
by you and flooded by the light
look, oh God, it crawls in
front of a taxidermy owl;
it'll live with all the low lives
without any grace it'll bow in
front of prophets who look
like midgets and harlequins
and its critics and wise men
the masters of logos and
arts promoters have become
eunuchs and governors
and when you die your dead
body, given to the sin, won't
ever find a piece of peaceful
soil to be buried, but it'll
remain a carcass left on earth

food for the dogs and serpents
leaving behind your legend
of a miserable skeleton that
no one wants to remember.

And when one morning
the God of love feel sorry
for you, and when salvation
comes for you, oh sinful soul,
you'll listen to the voice of
your redeemer and you'll
take off the cloths of shame
you'll again feel as light
as a bird and on the soil

you'll stir like a woman's
bosom, like a wave and having
no more steps to descend
the stairway of evil when
you'll be called again to rise
you'll feel the wings unfolding,
oh what a joy, your wings,
your great previous wings, oh Soul!

THE VIOLIN

The light came and the young man
recognized himself
            ~ D. Solomos

Their hands reversed your dress that excited
their fantasy. In your royal gown they defiled you,
the glorified, and they condemned you, the master.
                    ~ V. Hugo

In each child, in each dawn, the holy imagination
is reborn
                    ~Lenau

Day and night my mind
became such a sea wave.

Men of different races
call me a gypsy; the gypsies
call me of a different race
the workers call me lazy
the golden-hearted cry for me
the revellers don't want me
the healthy called me invalid
the invalid called me clown
dreamers looked at me with
strange eyes as if I started
an improper, foreign dream
as I pass the ghosts despise
my body and like a curse

the people avoid me; all
Christians and pagan cross
themselves when they see me
and if I resemble a tree and
multicoloured birds sing a
thousand songs among
my branches, hollow is
my trunk into which monkeys,
serpents and toads dwell; I
have freshness on my top
and poison deep in my roots.
I'm the shelter of none
no one ever leaned on me
the sky touches my face,
hell is hidden in my depth
I stand in the road's middle
like an obstacle, a scarecrow.
What are you waiting, oh
lumberjack, why you delay?
I'm not a tree, a corpse I am
of the rotten loner, a hole;
strike me, lumberjack, strike me
why you hesitate? No I haven't
sprouted out of the earth,
the dark earth has spat me out.

And where these thoughts
flood my mind, like an April
dawn in the deep green glen
I see something in front of
a cave, half buried in the soil
which was poking out like
a sprout, like a branch as if

it seek to say something though
the ivy tried to cover it again
and in the foggy sun rays
early in the morning, you
could see it like a hand, and other
times like a wounded little bird.

I lean down and grab the violin.

And the violin belonged to
the old anchorite and
I found it in front of his
lonely cave.

The old anchorite kept it
while he lived in the cave
with the rocks, the beasts
and with the ghosts

when he lived in peace
in constant contemplation
always having an eagle
companion by his side

when you looked at him
you felt deep inside of you
were there such people?
Aren't the gods dreams too?

And whether you were a
Turk, a gypsy, a holy man,
a hero or a thief you wished
to bow and pray before him.

In the cave where he lived
the anchorite kept untouched
unused and foreign
a violin among the violins

and he touched it from time to
time as the years passed
and all other old men said
that they sometimes heard

the glen echoing a godly
music as if the spouts
of heavens joined to
become one mouth

one heart so they could
sing all that the local hearts
couldn't tell and lips
couldn't disclose;

slowly the holy song spread
as rarely as ever and
was slowly absorbed
by the lonely glen

since the old anchorite
slowly ascended too
over the earth towards
the splendorous light.

As the years passed
the old man stopped using
his hands as if they remained
in the constant praying position

hands that never stirred
for any worthy movement
everything turned to marble
in the cold cave.

Then the old man vanished
I don't know where and when
he died or he ascended to
the heavens

and his companion eagle
also flew away from his side
and the violin, the most precious
treasure was left to me.

Play oh bow, play and
create a new world from
my hands in my two hands.
Oh a new race, oh you, new race
not the logos nor the song
not a sound from any mouth.
Only you exist, oh my violin
and there is only one tongue
and just one sound, yours,
which I, the player, create
and what creates the miracle
is none other but your music.

And if I'm a tree made
of chords and music
and nothing more, one sound
and one breath and one song
exist inside of me.

Oh opinion and oh concern,
oh logos I made your bed
just to remain awake
inside of me; become an ash
inside me, your concern, and
opinion, and logos, let the
whole world be dead. And
you sword, you bow, fall
onto the four pairs of chords
strike them, arouse them
let the harmony be heard

since the true world is
always created by the battle
between a bow and a chord
and whatever beautiful
existed, whatever harmonious
exists here in the mania
of a war is formed having
the victor as its father.

The musician gypsies came
and nested in my soul
and as you cut a bud here
and there some grass or leaf
and join them harmoniously
to make a tightly arranged
wreath, glory to the flower
arranger, thus from all
the sounds around me and
from the songs of my kin they
have placed my music onto
my violin like no other man.

And all other gypsies listened to
the songs, sounds and games
from all the violins of gypsies
slowly and timidly echoing
they revelled as if intoxicated
and they danced and celebrated
with those violins the sounds
of which they loved to absorb
but soon as they listened to my
prophetic song, my new flowery
creations they got excited and
they became very angry.

Men and women, young and old
while I the violin player stooped
and played with my hand that
was armed with the bow and
which travelled and burned and
flew and stroke and destroyed
and resurrected, created and
shone and sprouted onto the
four pairs of chords, the light-blue
diaphanous flower, my intact
soul was there too and chirped
like a violin.

Men and women, young and
old ran away from the violin
they didn't want to hear it again
plugging their ears they ran
and they pulled their hairs and
they cursed the violin player
and stoning him they laughed
with all mindless people and
they cursed all the irreverent.

And they said to one another:
Who's the one with the violin
who isn't pleasing our hearts
and inflames the surprise and
anger in our viscera? Who's
conniving with his unwise
hand awakening this violin
which talks of what we watch
it doesn't see and what we hold
it doesn't keep and in all
festivities and joys the anguish
stands before us like the traitor
of our kin and killer of our joy?

No other bow has ever played
such ugly, novice and imperfect
music on any gypsy violin
like the music of this foolish one.

And only the young children
oh the beloved children
filled my serene loneliness
turning it into my main fun
since my violin always
surprised and attracted them
and they run around me
with their big and bright eyes
into which they always
had hidden a tiny secret and
they made of all their surprise
and awe a great silence and joy
from my violin, the cursed
violin as if my own race,
from the far future time,

was gracing me with kisses
through these great kids.

They accompanied my song
with their big bright eyes and
I couldn't know from which
spring such pure music could
ever echo; from the shine of
their faces or the violin's soul?

Rejoice, oh, flower buds
of the first ever dawn as
you maintain the not spread
myrrh within your petals

and you eyes that you always
question, oh your not spread
wings, bodies nourished by
dreams, oh children with silky hair

you live in life's poverty
yet you feel over your
heads the soft caress
of the most softest hand

like the full moon which
spreads onto your hand and
asks you to keep it like
your younger little brother

and the dry yellow leaf
that is scattered in front of
your feet, you look at it as if
it is your little treasure

you can always match
the brightness of the sky
in the run of a little fawn and
in the quietness of the tree

oh freshly bloomed verdure
oh skies of all mothers
that you always exist
on the soil of the earth

since when and since once
you flawlessly heard
the most gracious and
harmonious sound

you possess the brave's
grace who kept listening to
the earth with his flawless
hearing he listened to

all the tidings coming
from afar and from
the underworld with
its over-worldly secrets.

OF RESURRECTION

If I'm Hades the destroyer
I'm Hades the creator
    ~ A. Valaoritis

Resurrection exists
only next to the graves
    ~ F. Nietzsche

Today you prepare something
great and unexpected and
you resemble the sun which
rises from the viscera of
the sea, firstly sprouted still
fresh and rosy-red stands
as if motionless and
indifferent glanced at by
many eyes, most gleaming
as it rises the world's master.

Today you prepare something
great and unexpected
though before you start your
sound a secret shiver
stirs your viscera. The bow
becomes an impatient soul
something better than
the sceptre of a king and
the wand of a witch; what

are you preparing, what
are you matching, oh
my creative violin?

Today you won't awake
one who's in deep sleep
today you won't only bring
a new dawn to the world
but you'll accomplish
something amazing: all
the immortals who have
died, those I buried myself
the immortals who have died
you'll bring to life with your
music of resurrection.

For this you have brought me
to the cemetery, here to wait
and for this all things around
here are joyous and bloomed
and rejoicing, which I've never
seen before around the graves
nor have I seen cypresses
so flexible like now, like
bodies that wish to embrace
and kiss like newlyweds.
And the graves are but tables
waiting to be set with flavourful
foods for crowned revellers
who'll come and feast until
the new rosy dawn comes.

And there among the graves
three sites were adorned with

gold and marble. The first
marble grave was for him
as if made of flesh, the all white,
blood shedding body; and there
was writing on top and on
the sides of the tomb as if it
was when the earth resembled
a queen during April and May.

And the second marble
grave was green and on it
the goddess of the sea was
depicted with enamel and
with pearls, the mermaid
with the fishes; And the grave
of the third man was the colour
of a lily and over this one
an image made by an artist
with wise hands who
designed the stary Heavens.

And you roll off the first
slab, oh my musical violin,
and love springs out of
the tomb like firstborn and
it re-blooms. And you roll off
the second gravestone, oh
violin, and behold here
our Motherland comes, thrice
revered among the revered
and you roll off the third
slab, oh my musical violin,
and behold all the Gods
come out of their darkness
all our Gods creating miracles.

Orchards bloom and open
their arms to Love, castles let
their thunder echo, here's
Motherland, rejuvenate all
you altars, now they all turn
immortal: the world creators
and the world creating Music.

I come from one motherland
even if I sometimes forget it
and I return to the one, I wish
to stand by it forever
wherever I might go to
whichever corner of the earth,
in nature or among people
in forlornness or in company

foreigner among foreigners
foreigner among my kin
riding a horse or walking
as much as I may forget it

without any effort of mine
I do care for it and all these
and every place I pass, each
lifetime I hastily spend

I still maintain inside me
dreams and shadows and
lighting bolts of my soul that
doesn't belong to any land
one thousand and two
homelands I had, which
talk to me a myriad words

which whether I feel or I don't
I still have as consolation.

And along the many lands
a precious beloved place
takes the soul of man
through his eyes and his hands

as wholesome and as bloomed
is this little tree only
in this land it blooms
better than in any other place

as the wax is made of
honey in the honeycomb
and as great people
live behind narrow fences

so long as the masters make
laws governed by logic
to control the people's wings
and tie down their feet

so long as in flowerless ravines
and on rocks with no verdure
in the orchards and
in the faraway skies

love is fed by hatred and
by anger and by war
and the Paradise is guarded
by the sword or by the fire

so long as the sun rays don't
warm up as they should

the multifaceted souls of the earth,
glory to homelands everywhere!

And above all motherlands
glory to you, my ideal
mountain peak, glorious
homeland, daughter of my music.

Your citizens drink your milk
the law abiding man lives with you
and the free man in his soul,
his life unfolds harmoniously

Justice is your crown
power is your sword
under your protection live
people, heroes and wise men.

You're meant to become
the daughter of music
nourishing all others
motherland of every race

nourished by the ethereal
breasts of heavenly ideals
you stir your flesh and blood
standing erect a diaphanous truth

orchards of lust, homeland of
castles, altars of gods and
all these and the immortal creator
is music, creator of the world.

The gods talked to me
and they said:

You buried us unjustifiably
you put us in deep graves
gods became ghosts and
tyrants became vampires

we, the sprouts of dreams
in this world
your life can't be spent
without us

though you deny us or
revere us, you shiver in fear or
curse us, you always
saunter under our shadows

all contemplation and
all paths lead to us and
we're presented as idols
as pneuma or as law.

We're the stirring vigil
of the night
they all shiver and keep silent
inexplicable like ghosts

We're true and virtuous
and beautiful
sitting on the highest throne
of Concept

we're the mist of foolishness,
the evil knives pulled
in the darkness of the night
companions of the stars

unwise, and wise, and god
fearing man with two opinions
godless, you always stumble
upon us, whoever you are

and no one can stir the heavens
that covers us and
whichever hand tries to stir
it freezes too

we're the rivers you can't
pass and the more
you drink of our water
the more thirsty you become

and you lean over our water
to admire your own image
and we all run like fools and
you think we're all alike

and when we dive deep into
the bowels of earth
again a mortal like you
pulls up into the sun

come now and lean over us
look at yourself
the wind blows you towards us
and your violin raises you.

Altars of the gods
castles of my homeland
orchards of lust
awake and immortal
oh you, world creator music

you awake the enchantress
maiden with doves of breasts
with your ordering words
towards the heavenly stars

and you leave your body
to decay in the tomb
while the grave was but
a salvation path for you

and you talk and turn gigantic
and you fly over the lands
while the stars place the fairy's
crown upon your head

and by your side I learn all
the secrets of nations and mortals
and all the apocrypha of
the cycles and of heavens

and all the risen worlds and
most beautiful maidens
in magical mirrors
I bring to you

my music becomes flesh
with our creating flames
excellent children are born
out of our eternal kisses

and with them the noble man
the last child and redeemer
most accomplished child of all
world creator, sincere.

And behold the ill-fated
man who rises victorious
onto a wide open earth, a
prophet with a wider soul.

Gold, precious stones, and
treasures, remains
of saints, the holy cross
every revered offering

all that come from the east and
west, from the south and north
I lay before your feet
that you can step on them

for one of your caresses I'll die a
thousand deaths, your precious
kiss, oh Love is worthy of
a thousand times redemption.

TALE OF THE TEARLESS

a colourful dream started in the imagination
~ Renan

Once upon a time there was a rich man
who had a son. Father and mother loved him;
he went to school; he learned of everything
that existed in the world
                    ~ (Beginning of a gypsy fairy tale)

A fairy tale occupies
the cave of my soul, a
tale that is tough like
lithos with strong words
like lead; a fairy tale
that crashes me

I don't know anymore, I
don't remember where I
heard it first or was it I who
experienced it once upon
a time? Yet whether you're
a stone, roll down to the cave
of my soul loudly and if
you're made of lead, melt
in the fire of the gypsy.

He had a father to whom
he was the precious one son

and he was like a star in
the tempest of the night

and they brought many
teachers to him who
taught him the best there was
the primal knowledge

and he felt as all the others
his heart that beat about
the Lord's contempt and
the heartlessness of the beast

and he cried at his parents
in a screeching piercing
voice "I'm the Tearless and
I demand", "Here my child
take these gold coins"

And soon the next day
with his empty hands:
"I'm the Tearless and I demand"
and they brought him gold

soon after again the one son
repeated and demanded
"I'm the Tearless please give me"
and they gave him possessions

"I'm the Tearless, bring more"
"Son we have no more gold coins"
"I have an abyss inside of me"
"Here my boy, here, take

the tool and bedding and
all you need, take the bread
from the counter and
the nail from the door"

And again he said, "I'm your
son and I always want"
"Here, take the house" they
said and he took it too.

When he demanded again the
two souls cried saying to him
"We only have our two bodies
do with them as you wish"

And he took them and
step by step he reached
the marketplace where he
sold them slaves, to you
oh king.

From the coins he got for
his mother he bought a golden
attire and from the silver
he got for his father he
gained an Arabian horse.

As the days passed and
they never saw him again
mother and father the slaves
missed their only son

the grief thus overtook them
the anguish of his loss

and the yearning to see him
again became a river of tears.

The king passed and asked them
"why you cry, you two slaves?"
"For our precious son, the
sun of every dawn

we cry for our precious son
who sold us for some coins
who exchanged us for gold
which you gave him oh king

and he hasn't come since then
our only joy and resolve"
and the king orders
"bring the boy in front of me"

"You're the destruction's son
and the ruin of your parents
and you're riding a horse
and you're dressed in all fanfare

tears you spread all over
tears you never had," "yes"
he answers and the king
writes an edict "noble son

take this edict and go away
become a lightning bolt and
for ten days and ten nights
don't you ever dare stop

go to the faraway lands of
my famous brother who
lives on the slopes of the
drenched in blood mountain

give him this edict, only
in the hands of my brother king
and wait" "Your order is my
command" he said and ran away.

Not the king's command
nor the slaves servitude
but the wing-whipped horse
took him away to his trip

he felt his destiny leading
him somewhere to
an unexpected end to
an unfamiliar spring

something inside him led
him, ordered him to travel
along deep crevasses and
the highest miracles and

he passed the endless plains
glens, rivers and woodlands
and he stepped on lands no
man had ever stepped

and his passing was like a
mind's that never stops
to anything but passed all
thoughts to create new

soon as it created one image
any soft idea softly
he traded all of them and
let the needless slide away

since he was going toward
the oceanic concern that
attracted him, where he wished
to dive his abyss-fed wings.

And from the immense desert
he came to pass riding his
black horse, dressed in his
snow white attire, with the
king's command written in
golden letters on a scroll,
like an enamel cup, he hid
in his bosom

and from the immense desert
he came to pass the fiery
forests that vanished in a cloud
of dust over which a flock
of crows flew and the eagles and
falcons flew over them too;

and the mistral was disturbed and
chatted with the reeds and
blackberry bushes and lower than
the foliage the snakes lurked
and a lizard basking in the sun
raised her head and cried aloud:
look at that!

and the green pastures were faraway
along with the flowering villages
and when each quietened down
in the embrace of the other,
from the groan of the camel
to the prayer of the muezzin,
when everything was left behind,
the thin skinned ascetic and
the slow passing of the caravan
that left behind a sweet
lengthened harmony and
the echo of colours and shadows
of female travellers with
undulating breasts, half covered
women with black eyes and
servants who followed helped by
their canes, tireless women
and the patriarch life that each
evening turned more holy and
blissful of which voyagers
sang with their tired voices.
And when he was left without
the company of passing wild
horses chased by the simoon
in the sunlit paths, the
Tearless felt a strange pain in
his viscera, the Ghost of thirst
that tyrannized him.

And it sprang out of rivers that
the desert mirage brought to
his feet, just an apparition
and he saw springs and oasis
foggy visions and untouchable

143

ghosts made of endless waters
for which his heart ached and
of which he constantly dreamed
and which he always desired
and which he never had.

Then his Arabian horse
turned his head and told him
the way seems fun to me
the libeccio is my food and
my follower is the desert fog
that rises under the fiery rays

trust me and let yourself
in my care, I'll look after you
since I see faraway where
your eyes can't discern;
let us go to the water that
is in front of us, there we'll go.

And he trusted his horse onto
which he leaned and they travelled
and he felt stronger as they went
and behold the small oasis
with golden palm trees, far
at the end of their path, in front
of his horse the deep water-well
sang softly

and thirst resided in its depths
like a black eye down in
the bottom shining and
looking up at the world, life

was undisturbed there in front
of his eyes

and he took the rope and he
wished to find a pitcher to drop
down and fetch some water

when his horse told him,
remember the scroll you hide
in your bosom; then he grabbed
the scroll, unrolled it and read
the written words: "kill the youth
that brings you this scroll, hell
vomited him and sent him
out to me; I want to kill him
but I can't. Tell me who is he
and why I tremble and my hand
can't do what is needed? Let it
be that by your hand this young
man has to die, my brother"

He wrapped the scroll again and
made a cup out of it, lowered it
in the water well and fetched
some water and his thirst
he quenched. Again he rode up
his horse that took him away

to a faraway land next to rivers
and lakes a country with many
castles that shone in the sun and
threatened the wide open skies;
there, he told his horse to stop.

And the king of that country
had the smileless as daughter
who was born to him by
a sprite who was his wife.

The daughter was beautiful,
and pretty like a thunderbolt,
restless like the wide sea and
all others which had destruction
in their breaths
and she was quiet like all
the deep and tough things

like the empty blue above us
like the marble that sparkles
in the sunshine

and she inherited her
mother's mind of a sprite
and she could solve riddles
indecipherable as if nature
couldn't hide anything
from her

and all who came to her
acquaintance, and all who
saw her fell in love and
as if pierced by Hades' spear
they all died.

Her father, the king,
announced his edict:
"Whoever wants Smileless
for a wife can come from

any part of the land but only
one who knows to tell her
a riddle she can't solve

and if she solves it
the would be groom is dead
and if she won't solve it he
can take her as his wife and
become my new son."

Many young men ran to
the challenge, the youth of
all the country, on foot and
riding their horses, princes
and men loaded with gold.

And magi came from Chaldean
lands, bureaucrats from Egypt
and the teachers from India,
wise men too from harmonious
Hellas

seers and prophets and
heroes and rhapsodists,
the highest of all and most
educated and many came
from the island of Thule

and all the suitors brought their
inexplicable riddles to her
all that belonged to
the Sphinx and Cybil and none
of them remained unexplained

and all the mouths which uttered
the riddles were swallowed by
the hungry Hades and she
walked over their bodies

the enchantress the riddle solver
who resembled a flowered
garden and gleamed flooded by
the light of the moon, she hid
earthquakes and lava in the coves
of her body;

yet the day came when the
chosen by Fate horse rider,
the tearless arrived a suitor
for the beautiful smileless

and behold here he is in front
of her, a groom to be and
challenger and you, oh
smileless wait here to
swallow him
and your eyes look like
deep holes where the fire
of Hades burns and all
the suitors who you've
annihilated, all you erased
from the face of the earth
they burn in there and you
exhume Medusa's breath.

Yet the Tearless doesn't see
and what he sees he takes
astride as he opens his mouth
to give you his riddle:

I rode on my father
I'm wearing my mother
to quench my thirst I
drank water with Hades

And you smileless freeze
and you're surprised and
you can't explain my
inexplicable riddle, here
I am your husband.

And for the first time ever
perhaps a master's arm
embraces your royal,
delicate body

was it the insolvable
riddle which puzzled you
or was it the graceful young
man to whom you bow?

And as you keep death
as your defence he too has
the insatiable lust that
attracts you to him

and you sob and cry
"oh my king, my father
I am your smileless
daughter and he's my man!"

The newlyweds are led to
their erotic bed where
hungry lust joins them
into an inseparable couple

149

and all erotic words echoed
in the darkened caves and
their nuptial song
was sang by virgin girls.

I rode on my father
I'm wearing my mother
to quench my thirst I
drank water with Hades

"My father awaits for us, oh
my beloved and the people
weave wreaths and crowns."
"My horse is neighing, oh
my love, ready to take us
away to our destiny"

"The throne is meant for us, oh
my beloved, the horns of war
and the lyres of peace are heard!"
"Voyages await for us, oh
my love, to unknown lands
to our first Fate together!"

"Let us stay here and have
children, oh my beloved, a new
world to our likeness!"
"Let us go, my love, to give
birth to the generation of tearless
which will change the world
in order to reach to this land
I turn my heart into stone and
I made a cemetery of my soul
I turn my mind into an arrow

and my wish into a ghost
I used all these starting with
my parents who I killed.

To my parents who grew old
and died blessing me, the
evil, let us go and build
a grave, and let's go and
put to the grave the evil king
who wanted me to die."

"Who's there standing
in front of me?", "I am
the one you dreamed of killing
but your dream didn't come
through, I have escaped
from the underworld.

I came back for you, oh king,
I carry the sword of revenge
I the tearless bring with me
the smileess Princess, the
gods of destruction paired us.

Mouth stop the talk, take charge
oh knife, behold, here is him
dead while his timid populace
cowardly offer me his crown

which I don't want; I didn't
return to become king of cowards
my people reside elsewhere
aloneness is my current throne

the seed of a thousand years
life stirs in the womb of my
beloved I am the trumpet
of resurrection, the stairway

that starts on earth and vanishes
among the stars, I'm the hand of
wisdom, I'm the tearless, my
diaphanous glance pierces time;

heartlessness and roughness
made me reach here very fast
I sold out my mom and dad
because of holy secret hunger

if the curse and sin of their deaths
sends me away, what of this?
You, oh tramplers, trample me
over so the pure wine will ferment.

I'm the Patriarch of my kin
which passes, unblemished and
courageous and foreign and
it goes and never stops and it
always seems unaltered and
slowly in the night it weaves
the world's new blanket.

The marks of its essence will
be incised all over its path
its joy will slowly intensify
like the joy of the tough, strong,
and tearless over lazy life
or enslaved.

All vanish in the circle of things
they go and return and although
they change they remain the same
and when the day will come when
they will all scatter away in an
earthquake, you, my children
will remain erect to uphold
the Universe.

Twelfth Narrative

THE WORLD

...Go to high mount Rhodope and to Haemus
where the north wind whips

~ Ovid

...seeing clearly the harmony of eternal nature that
never grows old and coming back to himself and
in whichever way...

~ Euripides

So little as it takes for
a thought to stir the mind
so little as it takes for
a sound to awake and to bring
soft and virgin words from
the depths of earth, the
trees talked to me and

the soft and sweetly-shaded
plain trees and the bulrushes
the flowered cedars and
the box-trees, the oaks and
all the ash trees and
the water loving lotuses
the myrtles and the oleanders
and the all over crawling ivy.
The tender reeds, the cypresses
the multicoloured rhododendrons

154

the fig trees the willows
that lean over the riverbanks
the blood dripping bearberry
the grapevines and the ferns
which resurrect people and
the beauty of a poplar.

And it was my soul's most
precious land somewhere
there at the Balkans
somewhere there at Rhodope.
Punished by the people
here I've come to you, oh
virgin forests, embrace me
and listen to my soul-violin.

And the trees told me: we know
of you, but your soul doesn't
like the soft words and fresh
dew which drips like honey
from our leaves and always talks
to the shepherds, the frontiersmen,
the couples with their kisses.

Yet our branches, flowers and
fruit, our fragrance and our birds
exhume words as if from our
sunless depths and these
words are only heard by those
who know how to read the secrets

while our roots, deep in earth's ,
bosom, suckle the fresh juice
from the nipples of mother

nature and bring her wisdom
directly to us; and what
we shall tell you is the Fate,
history and tradition of this earth.

In our memory you brought
our king, the most godly of gods
the creator of sounds: Orpheus
with his face and stature, with
his mind and lyre, here is the
life giving Thracean music.

He too, punished by the horrible
images of Hades, by the Sphinx
and by his desire for the virgin
Euridice, he too, exiled from life
and from joy came and said
"embrace me and listen to my music,
oh pure, innocent and great forests"

and we held him tightly in our
bosom and the sound of his
chirping lyre we took deep in
our hearts where it became our
dream and pure enchantment
and we became a temple and
he turned out to be a hymnist and
the prophet of God's harmony

and all creation around him from
the treetops to bottom grew up
and rose higher because of his
song; and the granite and old
boulders stirred too like bushes
and our bodies grew wings.

And from the roots to the outer
branches softly and sweetly
in our embrace he drank all
the blood of our hearts and
he learned the lesson of earth
and the old anguish disappeared
as he became the second
singer and creator of Olympus.

Though multifaceted nature is
one; the first youth of Olympus
has passed and in the second
the godly is exceptionally great
and we with you, oh Orpheus,
and all the other gods
become pneumas and
worship becomes a mystery
and religion a holy music.

And we don't know the powers
and of which abyss the demons
turned witches came together
and which hatred of Hades
conspired and slaughtered the
cantor Orpheus and the holy
lyre; and it was as if nature died
and the Earth became an orphan.

Which dream's shadow you've
tried to catch, which
beliefs you wish to establish,
which altar and which world?
Your violin pulls us upwards
beyond all dreams and

with our roots deep in the soil
we connect to mother earth.

Leave the dreams behind,
tune your ears listen to nature
solve the riddle of the rose and
make a Cybil out of a cypress.
Strike Chimera mercilessly
life is just a dream, let
your violin bring about
harmony among this truth.

Where is truth? Are you
perhaps lost in deep thoughts?
You can find the source of life
only inside you, oh human.

You can find it everywhere,
oh the ring of engagement,
between your heart and mind
and in all other forms of life.

Establish the third Olympus
place there the lonely too
and the smileless science;
which silver coin or smile
which gold resembles its face?

Shame on the fainthearted
Olympus, the heart is only
a miracle and the eyes
the miracle of the mind.
The world is lawless, debauched.
And the sun in the gleam

of the immense galaxy is
just a thin ray of light and
in the sun just discern a
flame in the chaos, and
behold: the Earth's flame
revolves in the ages and ages.

Under the inexplicable laws,
tightened together by steel,
the Earth for hours revolves
in circles and in the streets
while it dances the starry
dance of meditation as it
knows well whence it came
and where it's destined.

And it came about and it
lives and it might die too
but it won't ever stop in
the momentary cove of rest
since life always regains its
momentum by its own Power
an eternal path-follower and
always on its eternal road.

Before we existed the Earth
lived, before it spread its
plains it was alive with its
knowledge and wisdom;
in the primeval days water

and fire fought many
wars over the soft body
of this earth, and the two

enemy elements made
peace and lived together

and the world shone its joy
and purpose; you, oh
harmony, and the seed of
the great father stirred in
the womb of the endless sea
which gave birth to us too

and when the verdure of
the forests glowed with life
the world assumed a joyous,
unimaginable beauty. And
when man walked upon
the Earth his mind
shone like a new sun
that fogged the heavens.

And as the wars between
the elements and hatred end
then the lands and seas will
calm down so serenity and peace
will again shine in the souls
of human beings;

and supreme logos will survive
and people, and horses,
and the beasts like the trees
in the beautiful big forests.
The supreme final Fate
live, oh gypsy, upon your
most foreseeing violin.

KOSTIS PALAMAS (1859-1943)

Kostis Palamas, (13-01-1859 – 27-02-1943) was a Greek poet who wrote the words to the Olympic Hymn. He was a central figure of the Greek literary generation of the 1880s and one of the co-founders of the so-called New Athenian School along with Georgios Drosinis, Nikos Kampas, Ioanis Polemis.

Born in Patras, he received his primary and secondary education in Mesolonghi. In the 1880s, he worked as a journalist. He published his first collection of verses, *Songs of My Fatherland*, in 1886. He held an administrative post at the University of Athens between 1897 and 1926, and died during the German occupation of Greece during World War II. His funeral was a major event of the Greek resistance: the funerary poem composed and recited by fellow poet Angelos Sikelianos roused the mourners and culminated in an angry demonstration of a 100,000 people against Nazi occupation.

Palamas wrote the lyrics to the Olympic Hymn, composed by Spyridon Samaras. It was first performed at the 1896 Summer Olympics, the first modern Olympic Games. The Hymn was then shelved as each host city from then until the 1960 Winter Olympics commissioned an original piece for its edition of the Games, but the version by Samaras and Palamas was declared the official Olympic Anthem in 1958 and has been performed at each edition of the Games since the 1960 Winter Olympics.

The old administration building of the University of Athens, in downtown Athens, where his work office was located, is now dedicated to him and named *Kostis Palamas Building* and houses the *Greek Theater Museum*, as well as many temporary exhibitions.

He has been informally called the *national* poet of Greece and was closely associated with the struggle to rid Modern Greece of the *purist* language. He dominated literary life for 30 or more years and greatly influenced the entire political-intellectual climate of his time. Romain Rolland considered him the greatest poet of Europe and he was twice nominated for the Nobel Prize for Literature but never received it. His most important poem, *The Twelve Lays of the Gypsy* (1907), is a poetical and philosophical journey. His *Gypsy* is a free-thinking, intellectual rebel, a Greek Gypsy in a post-classical, post-Byzantine Greek world, an explorer of work, love, art, country, history, religion and science, keenly aware of his roots and of the contradictions between his classical and Christian heritages.

MANOLIS ALIGIZAKIS (1947–)

Emmanuel Aligizakis, (Manolis) is an apatris poet and author. He's the most prolific writer-poet of the diaspora with over 80 books published in more than a dozen different countries and in eleven different languages. At the age of eleven he transcribed the nearly 500 year old romantic poem Erotokritos, now released in a limited edition of 100 numbered copies and made available for collectors of such rare books at 5,000 dollars Canadian: the most expensive book of its kind to this day.

He was recently appointed an honorary instructor and fellow of the International Arts Academy, and awarded a Master's for the Arts in Literature. He is recognized for his ability to convey images and thoughts in a rich and evocative way that tugs at something deep within the reader. Born in the village of Kolibari on the island of Crete in 1947, he moved with his family at a young age to Thessaloniki and then to Athens, where he received his Bachelor of Arts in Political Sciences from the Panteion University of Athens.

After graduation, he served in the armed forces for two years and emigrated to Vancouver in 1973, where he worked as an iron worker, train labourer, taxi driver, and stock broker, and studied English Literature at Simon Fraser University. He has written three novels and numerous collections of poetry, which are steadily being released as published works.

His articles, poems and short stories in both Greek and English have appeared in various magazines and newspapers in

Canada, United States, Hungary, Slovakia, Romania, Australia, Jordan, Serbia and Greece. His poetry has been translated in Romanian, Swedish, German, Hungarian, Ukrainian, French, Portuguese, Arabic, Turkish, Serbian, Russian, Italian, Chinese, Japanese, languages and has been published in book form or in magazines in various countries.

He now lives in White Rock, where he spends his time writing, gardening, traveling, and heading Libros Libertad, an unorthodox and independent publishing company which he founded in 2006 with the goal of publishing literary books.

Following the steps of El Greco he finishes all his books with the phrase: *Μανώλης Αλυγιζάκης, Κρης εποίει*

His translation book "George Seferis-Collected Poems" was shortlisted for the Greek National Literary Awards the highest literary recognition of Greece. In September 2017 he was awarded the First Poetry Prize of the Mihai Eminescu International Poetry Festival, in Craiova, Romania.

He was nominated for the 2022 Nobel Prize in Literature by the Mihai Eminescu International Academy of Craiova, Romania.

His translation of "Tasos Livaditis – Poems, Volume II" was long listed for the 2023 Griffin Poetry Awards.

Nominated for the 2024 Zbigniew Herbert International Literary Awards, in Warsaw, Poland.

Μανώλης Αλυγιζάκης, άπατρις, εποίει

CONTENTS

Made in the USA
Columbia, SC
13 October 2024

43185527R00091